Understanding and Using WordPerfect

Patsy H. Lund
Lakewood Community College

Barbara A. Hayden

Sharon S. Larsen
Lakewood Community College

This book is available with or without the Student Version of WordPerfect® 4.2.

West Publishing Company
St. Paul   New York   Los Angeles   San Francisco

Credits: pp. 4, 15, 17, 22, 23, 34, 50, 51, 52, 63, 70, 71, 79, 80, 81, 82, 83, 101, 102, 113, 119, 128, 129, 131, 139, 154, 156, 158, 167, 170, 196, 197, 204, 205, 206, 212, 213. Courtesy of WordPerfect Corporation.

Copyeditor: John Thomas
Cover Design: Bob Anderson, Computer Arts, Inc.

Printed in the United States of America

Library of Congress Cataloging-in-Publication Data

Lund, Patsy H.
  Understanding and using WordPerfect.

  (The Microcomputing series)
  Includes index.
  1. Word processing. 2. WordPerfect (Computer
program)   I. Larsen, Sharon S. II. Hayden, Barbara A.
III. Title. IV. Series.
Z52.5.W65L86 1987   652'.5   86-26727
ISBN 0-314-30122-4
3rd Reprint—1988

ISBN 0-314-40883-5 (Student Version)

CONTENTS

Publisher's Note   xi
Preface   xiii
About the Authors   xv
Description of WordPerfect 4.2 Educational Software   xvi

PART 1   FUNDAMENTALS   1

UNIT 1   INTRODUCTION TO WORDPERFECT   3

Supplies Needed   3
Objectives   3
Assignments   4
WordPerfect   4
      The Template   4
      Menus   5
      The Quick Reference Card   5
      The User's Manual   5
Understanding and Using WordPerfect   6
      Conventions   6
Review Questions   7
Documentation Research   8

UNIT 2   CREATING YOUR FIRST DOCUMENT   11

Supplies Needed   11
Objectives   11
Important Keystrokes   12
Assignments   12
Using Appendix A   12
Formatting a Data Disk   13

Making a Copy of the Student Data Disk   13
Guided Activity: Loading WordPerfect   13
Loading WordPerfect into a Hard Disk System   14
The Status Line   14
Carriage Return   15
Hard Space   15
Soft Page   15
Hard Page   16
Guided Activity: Creating Your First Document   16
Saving Documents   16
Naming Documents   17
Guided Activity: Saving a Document   **17**
    The Importance of Saving Documents   **17**
The Cursor   18
    Cursor Movement Keys   **18**
    Horizontal Movement   18
    Vertical Movement   18
Go To   20
Saving a Document while Exiting WordPerfect   20
Guided Activity: Exiting WordPerfect   20
The Help Function   22
Guided Activity: Using the Help Screen   22
Retrieving a Document   23
Guided Activity: Retrieving a Document   23
Review Questions   24
Documentation Research   25

UNIT 3   TYPING AND PRINTING A BUSINESS LETTER   27

Supplies Needed   27
Objectives   27
Important Keystrokes   28
Assignments   28
Guided Activity: Creating a Business Letter   28
Editing a Document   30
Guided Activity: Editing a Business Letter   31
Toggle Keys   32
    The Insert Key   32
The Rewrite Feature   32
Guided Activity: Using the <TAB> and <INS> Keys   32
Guided Activity: Printing a Business Letter   33
Undelete   34
Review Questions   34
Documentation Research   36

APPLICATION A   37

UNIT 4   SIMPLE EDITING FUNCTIONS   43

Supplies Needed   43
Objectives   43

Important Keystrokes   44
Assignments   44
Enhancement Features   44
    The Bold Feature   44
    The Underline Feature   44
    Capitalization   44
    Centering Text   45
Guided Activity: Creating a Letterhead   45
The Flush Right Feature   47
Guided Activity: Inserting the Current Date Flush Right   47
The Block Feature   48
Guided Activity: Using the Block Feature to Enhance Existing Text   48
Menu   50
The Move and Copy Feature   50
Guided Activity: Moving a Block of Text   51
Append to File   52
The Block and Switch Features   52
Guided Activity: Using the Block and Switch Features   52
Guided Activity: Printing a Revised Business Letter   54
Reveal Codes   54
Guided Activity: Revealing Codes   56
Making Backup Copies of Your Documents   57
Review Questions   57
Documentation Research   58

UNIT 5 FORMATTING TEXT FOR PRINTING   61

Supplies Needed   61
Objectives   61
Important Keystrokes   62
Formatting Text for Printing   62

Section 1   62
Assignments   62
The Print Format Key   63
The Print Format Menu   63
Guided Activity: Copying a Block of Text   65
Guided Activity: Changing the Pitch   66
Guided Activity: Right Justification   67
Review Questions   68
Documentation Research   69

Section 2   70
Assignments   70
The Line Format Menu   70
Guided Activity: Setting Margins   72
Margin Release   74
Guided Activity: Changing Tab Settings   74
Guided Activity: Using Tab Settings   76
Guided Activity: Changing Line Spacing   76

Review Questions   78
Documentation Research   78

Section 3   79
Assignments   79
The Page Format Menu   79
Guided Activity: Creating Headers   84
Guided Activity: Changing the Page Number   85
Guided Activity: Inserting a Page Number at the Bottom Center of Each Page 86
Guided Activity: Using the Widow/Orphan Feature   86
Guided Activity: Centering a Page Vertically   87
Review Questions   88
Documentation Research   89

APPLICATION B   91

UNIT 6   CONTROLLING THE PRINTER   99

Supplies Needed   99
Objectives   99
Important Keystrokes   99
Assignments   100
Printing   100
The Print Menu   100
Guided Activity: Printing Two Copies of a Single Page   103
Guided Activity: Printing a Block of Text   104
Guided Activity: Stopping and Restarting a Print Job   105
Guided Activity: Printing a Document Stored on a Data Disk   106
Guided Activity: Cancelling a Print Job   107
Review Questions   108
Documentation Research   109

UNIT 7   DISCOVERING MORE WORDPERFECT FUNCTIONS   111

Supplies Needed   111
Objectives   111
Important Keystrokes   112
Assignments   112
Default Values   112
The Date and Time Feature   112
    The Date Menu   112
Guided Activity: Inserting the Date and Time Automatically   114
Indenting   115
Guided Activity: Typing a Paragraph   115
Guided Activity: Indenting Text from the Left Margin   115
Guided Activity: Indenting Text from the Right and Left Margins   116
Guided Activity: Creating a Hanging Paragraph   116
Repeating a Character or Feature   117
Guided Activity: Using the Repeat Feature   117
Superscripts and Subscripts   119
Guided Activity: Using Superscripts   120

Guided Activity: Using Subscripts   120
Guided Activity: Using the Advance Down Feature   122
Search and Replace   123
    Search   123
    Replace   125
Guided Activity: Searching Up and Down   125
Guided Activity: Automatic Search and Replace   127
Footnotes and Endnotes   129
Guided Activity: Creating Footnotes   130
The Tab Ruler   131
Guided Activity: Displaying the Tab Ruler   132
Split Screen   133
Review Questions   134
Documentation Research   135

UNIT 8   FILE MANAGEMENT   137

Supplies Needed   137
Objectives   137
Important Keystrokes   138
Assignments   138
File Management   138
Guided Activity: Using List Files to Retrieve a Document   140
Guided Activity: Using List Files to Print a Document   140
Guided Activity: Using List Files to Look at a File   141
Guided Activity: Using List Files to Rename a File   141
Guided Activity: Using List Files to Delete a File   141
Locked Documents   142
Review Questions   142
Documentation Research   143

APPLICATION C   145

PART 2 SPECIAL FEATURES   151

UNIT 9   SPELLER AND THESAURUS   153

Supplies Needed   153
Objectives   153
Important Keystrokes   154
Assignments   154
The Speller   154
The Check Menu   154
The Not Found Submenu   155
The Double Word Submenu   156
Guided Activity: Spell-Checking   157
The Thesaurus   158
Guided Activity: Using the Thesaurus   159
Review Questions   162
Documentation Research   162

UNIT 10   MERGING   163

Supplies Needed   163
Objectives   163
Important Keystrokes   164
Assignments   164
Merging   164
The Secondary File   165
Guided Activity: Creating a Secondary File   165
The Primary File   167
Guided Activity: Creating a Primary File   167
Merging and Printing   169
Guided Activity: Merging and Printing a Personalized Letter   170
Mailing Labels   171
Guided Activity: Creating a Primary File for Mailing Labels   171
Guided Activity: Merging Files to Print Mailing Labels   172
Formatting Mailing Labels   173
Guided Activity: Printing Mailing Labels   173
More On Merging   174
Guided Activity: Creating a Secondary File   175
Guided Activity: Linking Secondary Files   175
Review Questions   176
Documentation Research   177

UNIT 11   MACROS   179

Supplies Needed   179
Objectives   179
Important Keystrokes   179
Assignments   180
Macros   180
Guided Activity: Creating a Permanent Macro to Print a Document   180
Guided Activity: Creating a Macro to Store Margin Settings   182
Guided Activity: Creating a Macro That Contains Text   183
Guided Activity: Retrieving a Macro   184
Guided Activity: Creating a Macro Chain   185
Guided Activity: Using a Macro Chain   186
Review Questions   186
Documentation Research   187

APPLICATION D   189

UNIT 12   COLUMNS   195

Supplies Needed   195
Objectives   195
Important Keystrokes   195
Assignments   196
Text Columns   196
The Math/Columns Menu   196
Guided Activity: Creating a Newspaper Column   197

Guided Activity: Creating Parallel Columns   199
Review Questions   201
Documentation Research   202

UNIT 13   TABLE OF CONTENTS, LISTS, AND INDEXES   203

Supplies Needed   203
Objectives   203
Important Keystrokes   203
Assignments   204
Tables of Contents, Lists, and Indexes   204
Marking Text   204
Guided Activity: Creating a Table of Contents   207
Review Questions   209
Documentation Research   209

UNIT 14   MATH   211

Supplies Needed   211
Objectives   211
Important Keystrokes   211
Assignments   212
The Math Feature   212
The Math Definition Menu   212
Guided Activity: Setting Tabs   214
Guided Activity: Defining Columns   214
Guided Activity: Creating a Budget Worksheet   215
Guided Activity: Calculating the Budget Worksheet   218
Guided Activity: Turning Off the Math Feature   220
Review Questions   220
Documentation Research   221

APPLICATION E   223

APPENDIX A   GETTING STARTED ON YOUR MICROCOMPUTER   A-1

APPENDIX B   ANSWERS TO CHECKPOINT QUESTIONS   B-1

APPENDIX C   WORDPERFECT VERSION 4.2   C-1

INDEX   I-1

QUICK REFERENCE

PUBLISHER'S NOTE

This book is part of THE MICROCOMPUTING SERIES. We are proud to announce that this unique series is now entering its third year, and currently includes four different types of books:

1. A core concepts book, now in its second edition, teaches basic hardware and software applications concepts. This text is titled UNDERSTANDING AND USING MICROCOMPUTERS.

2. A series of introductory level, hands-on workbooks for a wide variety of specific software packages. These provide both self-paced tutorials and complete reference guides. Each book's title begins with UNDERSTANDING AND USING . . . .

3. Several larger volumes combine DOS with three popular software packages. Two of these volumes are called UNDERSTANDING AND USING APPLICATION SOFTWARE, while the third is titled UNDERSTANDING AND USING SHAREWARE APPLICATION SOFTWARE. These versions condense components of the individual workbooks while increasing the coverage of DOS and the integration of different application packages.

4. An advanced level of hands-on workbooks with a strong project/systems orientation. These titles all begin with DEVELOPING AND USING . . . .

Our goal has always been to provide you with maximum flexibility in meeting the changing needs of your courses through this "mix and match" approach. We remain committed to offering the widest variety of current software packages.

We now offer these books in THE MICROCOMPUTING SERIES:

Understanding and Using Microcomputers, second edition   by Steven M. Zimmerman and Leo M. Conrad

OPERATING SYSTEMS

Understanding and Using MS-DOS/PC DOS:
The First Steps
    by Laura B. Ruff and Mary K. Weitzer

Understanding and Using MS-DOS/PC DOS:
A Complete Guide
    By Cody T. Copeland and Jonathan P. Bacon

PROGRAMMING LANGUAGES

Understanding and Using Microsoft BASIC/IBM-PC BASIC
    by Mary L. Howard

WORD PROCESSORS

Understanding and Using Displaywrite 3 and Displaywrite 4
    by Patsy H. Lund and Barbara A. Hayden

Understanding and Using Microsoft Word
    by Jonathan P. Bacon

Understanding and Using MultiMate
    by Mary K. Weitzer and Laura B. Ruff

Understanding and Using PC-Write
    by Victor P. Maiorana

Understanding and Using pfs:WRITE
    by Mary K. Weitzer and Laura B. Ruff

Understanding and Using WordPerfect
    by Patsy H. Lund, Barbara A. Hayden,
    and Sharon S. Larsen

Understanding and Using WordStar
    by Steven C. Ross

Understanding and Using WordStar 4.0
    by Patsy H. Lund and Barbara A. Hayden

SPREADSHEET PACKAGES

Understanding and Using ExpressCalc (Including PC-CALC)
    by Victor P. Maiorana and Arthur A. Strunk

Understanding and Using Lotus 1-2-3
    by Steven C. Ross

Understanding and Using Lotus 1-2-3 Release 2
    by Steven C. Ross

Understanding and Using SuperCalc 3
    by Steven C. Ross and Judy A. Reinders

Understanding and Using SuperCalc 4
    by Judy A. Reinders and Steven C. Ross

DATABASE PACKAGES

Understanding and Using dBASE III (Including dBASE II)
    by Steven C. Ross

Understanding and Using dBASE III PLUS
    by Steven C. Ross

Understanding and Using PC-FILE III
    by Victor P. Maiorana and Arthur C. Strunk

Understanding and Using pfs: FILE/REPORT
    by Laura B. Ruff and Mary K. Weitzer

Understanding and Using R:BASE 5000
(Including R:BASE System V)
    by Karen L. Watterson

INTEGRATED SOFTWARE

Understanding and Using Appleworks (Including AppleWorks 2.0)
    by Frank Short

Understanding and Using Educate-Ability
    by Victor P. Maiorana and Arthur A. Strunk

Understanding and Using FRAMEWORK
    by Karen L. Watterson

Developing and Using Office Applications with AppleWorks
    by M. S. Varnon

Understanding and Using Symphony
    by Enzo V. Allegretti

COMBINATION VOLUMES

Understanding and Using Application Software, Volume 1:
DOS, WordStar 4.0, Lotus 1-2-3 Release 2, and dBASE III Plus
    by Patsy H. Lund, Barbara A. Hayden, and Steven C. Ross

Understanding and Using Application Software, Volume 2:
DOS, WordPerfect, Lotus 1-2-3 Release 2, and dBASE III Plus
    by Patsy H. Lund, Barbara A. Hayden, and Steven C. Ross

Understanding and Using SHAREWARE Application Software:
DOS, PC-Write, ExpressCalc, and PC-FILE
    by Victor P. Maiorana and Arthur A. Strunk

ADVANCED BOOKS

Developing and Using Advanced Lotus 1-2-3 Applications
    by Steven C. Ross

Developing and Using Decision Support Applications
    by Steven C. Ross, Richard J. Penlesky, and Lloyd D. Doney

Developing and Using Micrcomputer Business Systems
    by Kathryn W. Huff

We are delighted by the popularity of THE MICROCOMPUTING SERIES. We appreciate your support, and look forward to your suggestions and comments. Please write to us at this address:

West Publishing Company
College Division
50 West Kellogg Blvd. P.O. Box 64526 St. Paul, MN 55164

PREFACE

As microcomputer use increases in academic and workplace settings, so also does the demand for well-designed application software. WordPerfect was designed in response to the practical need to produce a variety of professional documents quickly and accurately. It is a sophisticated software package with extensive capabilities. Each word-processing task, however, has unique requirements, and therefore only some of WordPerfect's features are needed to produce an individual document. Consequently, WordPerfect is arranged so that each feature can be accessed individually, just when it is needed.

Understanding and Using WordPerfect is also designed to meet the needs of individuals who have unique word-processing tasks. It is arranged to guide the user through a step-by-step process in understanding how to use each of WordPerfect's features. It examines both the fundamental and the sophisticated word-processing capabilities of WordPerfect. This workbook itself is an illustration of WordPerfect's capabilities; it was both written and formatted with the WordPerfect word-processing package.

Each unit contains

> **Objectives** that list the skills you will acquire.

> **Important Keystrokes** that summarize the commands you will use.

> **Guided Activities** that present step-by-step instructions for using individual WordPerfect features.

> **Computer screens** that illustrate the menus that activate specific features.

> **Checkpoints** that test your understanding of the Guided Activities.

> **Review Questions** that test your understanding of the information contained in each unit.

> **Documentation Research** that guides you in examining the WordPerfect user's manual.

Additional features of Understanding and Using WordPerfect include

> **Applications** you can use to apply your acquired skills.

Quick Reference, on the last pages of the workbook, a list of the most frequently used commands.

Appendix A (Getting Started on Your Microcomputer), a reference for using an IBM PC or compatible computer to run the WordPerfect program.

Appendix B, answers to Checkpoints.

Appendix C, a description of updated features for WordPerfect 4.2 users.

WordPerfect Student Data disk with student files, which will be used for some of the Guided Activities.

NOTICE

The educational limited-use version of WordPerfect which accompanies this text is version 4.2. The changes between WordPerfect 4.1 and 4.2 are minimal and students will have no difficulty in performing all of the exercises and applications in the text using the limited-use version 4.2. This text has been modified to take in the effects of version 4.2 through the appendix.

ACKNOWLEDGMENTS

The authors of <u>Understanding and Using WordPerfect</u> acknowledge the efforts of the following people in the production of this workbook. Many thanks to

Burnette Foss, Jay Ramsperger, and Alicia Wiggins, who did a superb job typing and proofreading the manuscript.

Lee Schomaker, president of Alpha Associates, for his encouragement and support.

Rich Wohl, editor of **The MICROCOMPUTING SERIES**, for his confidence in our ability to write and produce this book.

Cheryl Wilms, production assistant, and John Thomas, copyeditor, for their assistance and patience.

Charles F. Parker, Lansing Community College; David L. Anderson, Wheaton College; Sandra S. Belisle, Mesa Community College; and Linda Belford, Pittsfield High School; for finding the time to respond to this manuscript.

WordPerfect Corporation, for producing a software package with the capability to write this workbook.

Our families, whose generosity and good humor meant a great deal to the successful completion of this project.

ABOUT THE AUTHORS

Patsy H. Lund earned her Bachelor of Arts degree from Metropolitan University in St. Paul, Minnesota, and her M.B.A. from the College of St. Thomas in St. Paul. Her professional experience includes microcomputer training on IBM and IBM compatibles and technical writing for curriculum development.

Patsy is currently a college instructor, with teaching experience in the areas of accounting, computer science, and data processing, at Lakewood Community College, White Bear Lake, Minnesota. She is also the Vice President of Administration and Finance for Alpha Associates, St. Paul, Minnesota.

Sharon P. Larsen earned her Bachelor of Arts degree from St. Olaf College in Northfield, Minnesota. She is currently enrolled in the Master of Administration and Management program at Metropolitan State University in St. Paul, Minnesota. Her professional experience includes microcomputer training on IBM and IBM compatibles and technical writing for curriculum development.

Sharon is currently a college instructor, with experience in the areas of computer science, data processing, and office automation, at Lakewood Community College in White Bear Lake, Minnesota. She is also the Vice President of Operations for Alpha Associates, St. Paul, Minnesota.

Barbara A. Hayden earned her Bachelor of Science degree in education from the University of Maryland, College Park, Maryland. She is currently enrolled in the Master of Business Communications program at the College of St. Thomas in St. Paul, Minnesota. Her professional experience includes elementary education and freelance and technical writing. She is currently a software consultant at Alpha Associates in St. Paul, Minnesota.

```
TO:     Users of the Limited-Use version of WordPerfect 4.2
FROM:   Wordperfect Corporation
RE:     The limitations of Limited-Use Wordperfect 4.2
DATE:   June 30, 1987
        ***********************************************************
```

The Limited-Use introductory version of WordPerfect 4.2 (L-WP) is intended to allow one to <u>learn</u> the features of WordPerfect 4.2; however, the L-WP is not intended to allow one to print usable academic or professional documents**.

Certain limitations which should not deter <u>learning</u> WordPerfect through the L-WP have been encrypted into the L-WP to guard against productive use, and are as follows:

I.   One may work with as large a document on screen as desired, but one may only save to disk a data file no larger than 50,000k (approximately 25-30 regular pages).

      1. A data file created with the L-WP cannot be imported into regular WordPerfect, nor can a file created in regular WordPerfect be imported into L-WP.

II.   Data files of any size may be printed through parallel printer port "1" without defining a printer, but font changes and extended ASCII characters are not allowed. Also, **"*WPC"** will be printed after each paragraph.

III. One will be able to learn all the functions of WordPerfect 4.2's speller and thesaurus by calling up the "readme.wp" and following the step-by-step directions; however, one cannot use the L-WP speller and thesaurus with any of one's own documents because there are only a limited number of words in the L-WP speller and thesaurus. (The regular speller has 115,000 words, and the regular thesaurus has approximately 150,000 words.)

IV.   The help file of L-WP allows the user to retrieve the function-key template, but similar to the speller and the thesaurus described above, the space will not allow the full help files on the L-WP disk.

L-WP is designed to be used for introductory, word processing courses and thus far has been well received in these types of environments. Notwithstanding the broad abilities provided in the L-WP, presumably the L-WP will not satisfactorily substitute for regular WordPerfect 4.2, and therefore the full feature version may be obtained directly from WordPerfect Corporation via the enclosed order form at a 75% educational discount.

     **"*WPC" will be automatically printed after each paragraph of text to discourage academic or professional use of the L-WP.

1

FUNDAMENTALS

UNIT

1

INTRODUCTION TO WORDPERFECT

SUPPLIES NEEDED

1. WordPerfect user's manual
2. WordPerfect Quick Reference card
3. WordPerfect keyboard template

OBJECTIVES

After completing this unit, you will be able to

1. use the Table of Contents and the Index to find information in the user's manual;
2. use the template to identify the purpose of each function key;
3. use the Quick Reference card to become familiar with the features that specific keystrokes activate.

ASSIGNMENTS

1. Review Questions
2. Research Documentation

WORDPERFECT

WordPerfect is a software package that is capable of performing both simple and complex word processing tasks. It consists of five disks, a program disk, the Speller, the Thesaurus, the Printer, and the Learning disk. The package also contains a keyboard template, a Quick Reference card, and a user's manual.

The Template

The plastic keyboard template (Figure 1-1) fits over the ten function keys at the left of the IBM PC keyboard. A template is also available for those keyboards on which the function keys are located in a row across the top.

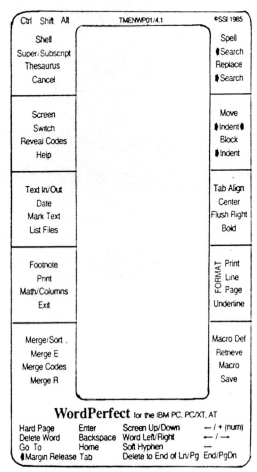

FIGURE 1-1 WordPerfect Keyboard Template.

The template identifies the purpose of each of the function keys located on the keyboard. Used in combination with the Alt, Shift, and Ctrl keys, these ten keys activate fifty WordPerfect features. The template makes it easier to remember those functions. To make it even easier, the template is color coded.

The color codes are defined as follows:

BLACK Press the function key.

BLUE   Hold down Alt while pressing the function key.

GREEN Hold down Shift while pressing the function key.

RED   Hold down Ctrl while pressing the function key.

Study the template and the features offered by WordPerfect. As you learn to use WordPerfect, associating each key with the function it performs will become automatic.

Menus

WordPerfect is designed to access a menu each time a function key is pressed. Each menu offers a list of options that allows you to select a particular WordPerfect feature. Menus simplify operations, save time, and reduce data-entry errors. WordPerfect is designed to keep menus out of sight until they are actually needed, thus increasing word-processing efficiency.

The Quick Reference Card

The Quick Reference card lists WordPerfect's features along with the keystrokes that activate those features. It also lists the cursor control keys, which are used to move you quickly and easily through the pages of the documents you create.

The Quick Reference card also provides information on starting WordPerfect, saving documents, clearing the screen, and exiting the program. It includes a picture of the IBM keyboard and an explanation of the color coding system.

The User's Manual

The WordPerfect user's manual is divided into eight sections. This manual is an indispensable part of the WordPerfect package, for it documents all the program's features. It is, at first sight, an overwhelmingly large document, but you will learn to use it to look up those particular features that are relevant to your needs.

The first section is entitled Getting Started. Use it to find basic information about WordPerfect software and simple explanations of procedures you need to get started.

The second section is entitled Learning. It consists of twelve lessons to teach you about WordPerfect's features. Use it in combination with the Learning disk.

The third section is the Reference section. It contains an alphabetical listing of WordPerfect features along with an easy-to-follow explanation of how to activate each feature. Use this section regularly. It is arranged to help you find basic information with minimal effort.

The fourth section contains information on the Speller and Thesaurus. Use it to learn the specifics of these features.

The fifth section is entitled Special Features. Use it to find out about WordPerfect's special capabilities, such as producing newspaper columns, outlines, or tables of contents.

The sixth section, entitled Merge, contains information on merging two or more documents.

The seventh section, entitled Math, contains information about calculations that you can perform with WordPerfect.

The eighth section, the Glossary/Index, contains a glossary of WordPerfect terms and a comprehensive index.

UNDERSTANDING AND USING WORDPERFECT

This workbook is divided into two parts. Part 1, Fundamentals, teaches you to create, revise, and print a document. It also teaches you to manage your documents (files).   After you have completed Part 1, you will be able to use WordPerfect to produce memos, reports, business letters, and manuscripts.

Part 2, Special Features, teaches you about WordPerfect's special capabilities, such as merging, math, and keystroke programming (macros). It also teaches you to use the Speller and the Thesaurus.

Conventions

Several typographical conventions have been established to improve readability and understanding. They were established to clearly communicate each WordPerfect function. They are as follows:

> When a keystroke activates a single command, it is designated like this: <KEYNAME> (e.g., <CR>, <SPACEBAR>).

> The keys that direct cursor movement are designated, for example, like these: <Up>, <Down>, <Left>, <Right>, <Home>, <End>, <PgUp>.

When one key is used in combination with another, the first one must be held down while the other is pressed. Combination keys are separated by a hyphen (e.g., Alt-F4).

When keys are pressed one after another but not in combination, they are separated by a comma (e.g., <Home>,<Home>,<Right> arrow).

All functions begin with a capital letter (e.g., Exit, Save, Cancel).

REVIEW QUESTIONS

1. Explain how WordPerfect's keyboard template is used.

2. Which section of the user's manual provides lessons on using the features contained in WordPerfect?

3. Assume that you have used WordPerfect to create a memo but have forgotten which key to press to use the Save function. How can you quickly look this up?

4. Explain WordPerfect's color coding system.

5. Which section of the user's manual (documentation) will you use to find information on starting the WordPerfect program?

DOCUMENTATION RESEARCH

1. Locate the Glossary/Index section in the user's manual, then use the glossary to define the following terms:

    Boot

    Cursor

Default Drive

Document

Editing

Enter key

Hard disk

Memory

Menu

Monitor

RAM

String

Write Protect

2. Locate the Reference section in the user's manual, then look up the
    description of each of the following:

    Cancel

    _____

    Flush Right

    _____

    Typeover

    _____

    Capitalization

    _____

3. Locate the Getting Started section in the user's manual, then describe the
    following:

    5 Keys to Know

    _____

    Conventions

    _____

    The Template

    _____

UNIT

2 CREATING YOUR FIRST DOCUMENT

SUPPLIES NEEDED

1. disk operating system (DOS) disk
2. WordPerfect program disk
3. WordPerfect Learning disk
4. two data disks
5. Understanding and Using WordPerfect Student Data disk

OBJECTIVES

After completing this unit you will be able to

1. load the WordPerfect program;
2. format a data disk;
3. create and name a one-page document;
4. save a document on your data disk in designated drive;
5. retrieve a document;
6. use the "status line" to identify your position in a document;
7. use the cursor keys to move within a document;
8. use the <CR> key;
9. exit WordPerfect.

IMPORTANT KEYSTROKES

1. F10.....................................saves a document
2. F7......................................saves a document and exits WordPerfect
3. Shift-F10..............................retrieves a document
4. F3......................................invokes Help screen
5. F1......................................cancels feature just activated
6. Ctrl-<Home>............................move cursor to specific location
7. Cursor movement keystrokes:

   Horizontal Movement

   <Right> arrow key..................moves cursor one character to the right
   <Left> arrow key....................moves cursor one character to the left
   Ctrl-<Right> arrow keys.............move cursor one word to the right
   Ctrl-<Left> arrow keys..............move cursor one word to the left
   <Home>,<Right> arrow keys..........move cursor to the right edge of the screen
   <Home>,<Left> arrow keys...........move cursor to the left edge of the screen
   <Home>,<Home>,<Right> arrow keys...move cursor to the end of the line
   <Home>,<Home>,<Left> arrow keys....move cursor to the beginning of the line

   Vertical Movement

   <Up> arrow key.....................moves cursor one line up
   <Down> arrow key...................moves cursor one line down
   <Home>,<Up> arrow keys.............move cursor to the top of the screen
   <Home>,<Down> arrow keys...........move cursor to the bottom of screen
   <Home>,<Home>,<Up> arrow keys......move cursor to the beginning of the document
   <Home>,<Home>,<Down> arrow keys....move cursor to the end of the document
   <PgUp> key.........................moves cursor to top of current page
   <PgDn> key.........................moves cursor to the bottom of current page

ASSIGNMENTS

1. Create **Forfun**
2. Save **Forfun**
3. Practice Cursor Movement
4. Exit WordPerfect
5. Retrieve **Forfun**
6. Review Questions
7. Research Documentation

USING APPENDIX A

Appendix A contains information about your microcomputer and the disk operating system (DOS). It provides specific information about the keyboard, startup and shutdown procedures, specific commands, file naming, directory use, and document printing. By referring to this appendix, you will be able to use the WordPerfect program to perform the tasks in this workbook.

FORMATTING A DATA DISK

Your instructor will supply a copy of the DOS disk. Your first task is to use the DOS disk to format two blank disks, which will be used to store the documents you are going to create. Refer to Appendix A and follow the steps to format a disk.

When the task of formatting is complete, use a felt-tip pen to label your disks "WordPerfect Student Data".

MAKING A COPY OF THE STUDENT DATA DISK

Your instructor will lend you a copy of the Understanding and Using WordPerfect Student Data disk. It contains the documents (files) you will edit as you follow the Guided Activities in this book. Copy the Understanding and Using WordPerfect Student Data disk onto both of the disks you formatted. You will then have one disk to work with and one disk for backup. Follow the steps in Appendix A to Copy.

Be sure to return both the DOS and the Understanding and Using WordPerfect Student Data disks to your instructor.

GUIDED ACTIVITY: LOADING WORDPERFECT

Refer to Startup Procedures in Appendix A to perform the following task:

1.   Insert the WordPerfect program disk into Drive A.
     Insert the WordPerfect Student Data disk into Drive B.

     A prompt to enter the current date will appear, followed by a prompt to enter the current time.

2.   Enter the date and time.

     An A> (A prompt) will appear.

3.   Type "B:".

     Your screen will look like this: A>B:

     You have indicated that your documents will be stored on a disk in Drive B.

4.   Press the <CR> key.

     Your screen will look like this: B>

5.   Type "A:WP".

     Your screen will look like this: B>A:WP

6.   Press the <CR> key.

The WordPerfect logo will be briefly displayed, then a clear screen will appear. The clear screen is the typing area on which you will create your document. Right now, it contains only a status line at the bottom of the screen.

✔ CHECKPOINT

a.   How does pressing <CR> after A>B: affect what appears on the screen?

═══

b.   Into which drive do you insert your WordPerfect Student Data disk?

═══

What You Have Accomplished

You have succeeded in loading the WordPerfect program into your computer. You have also designated Drive B to store the documents that you will create. If you do not designate a separate drive on which to store your documents, they will be stored instead on the WordPerfect program disk, on which there is little available space.

LOADING WORDPERFECT INTO A HARD DISK SYSTEM

The procedure for loading WordPerfect into a hard disk system differs from the procedure used to load it into a single or dual drive system. Assume that your hard disk has already been formatted and is storing the necessary DOS files. Follow the Startup Procedures for a hard disk system in Appendix A. A C> (C prompt) will appear. Insert the WordPerfect program disk into Drive A. Type "A:wp" after the C>, then press <CR> to load the WordPerfect program.

THE STATUS LINE

The status line (Figure 2-1) is displayed in the lower right corner of the screen. The status line states (from left to right) the current document number and the page number, line number, and column (position) number at which the cursor is presently located. The status line also displays messages from the program or from DOS.

The Doc (document) number indicates the number of the document currently being edited. Notice that the status line on your screen displays "Doc 1". Unless you are using the Split Screen Feature, which allows you to edit two documents simultaneously, this line will display "Doc 1".

The Pg (page) number identifies the number of the page currently being edited. The page number changes as you move the cursor through the pages of the documents you create. You are currently on Pg 1.

The Ln (line) number identifies the specific line of the page on which you are entering text. A standard page of text contains fifty-four lines. Only twenty-four of those lines are displayed on your screen at one time. When you enter text beyond Ln 24, the lines of your document scroll off the top of your screen, one at a time. When you reach the end of a page, a dotted line appears across the screen.

The Pos (position) number identifies the column number or horizontal space at which the cursor is located. When you type a line, the position number changes as the cursor moves across the page.

Doc 1 Pg 1 Ln 1 Pos 10

FIGURE 2-1 Clear Screen with Status Line.

CARRIAGE RETURN

The purpose of a carriage return <CR> within a word-processing program is different from its purpose on a conventional typewriter. When you enter text on a screen and come to the end of a line, the program automatically wraps text around to the next line. Therefore, the only time it is necessary to press <CR> is when you want to begin a new line before you reach the end of the line you are currently on, as when you wish to begin a new paragraph. The <CR> key is also used to insert a blank line. If you press <CR> at the beginning of a line you will insert a blank line into the text. You should also press <CR> when you have reached the end of your document.

HARD SPACE

Sometimes it is necessary to keep two or more words together on a line. When this occurs, insert a Hard Space by pressing <Home>,<SPACEBAR> between the words you wish to keep together.

SOFT PAGE

When a page is filled with text, WordPerfect automatically inserts a page break. A dotted line appears on the screen to indicate the end of one page and the beginning of another. The cursor jumps to the next page, and a new page number appears in the status line.

HARD PAGE

To end a page before it is filled with text, press the Ctrl-<CR> keys. A dotted line appears on your screen to indicate the end of one page and the beginning of another. The cursor jumps to the new page. If you want to delete this hard page break, move the cursor below the page break line and press <BACKSPACE>.

GUIDED ACTIVITY: CREATING YOUR FIRST DOCUMENT

Type the document shown in Figure 2-2. Do not bother to correct typing errors now. Remember that you do not need to press <CR> at the end of a line.

> Type this document exactly as you see it. Notice that when you reach the right margin, a new line is automatically started. If a word is too long to fit at the end of a line, it "wraps" around the screen and becomes the first word in the next line. This feature of the WordPerfect program is called "word wrap."
>
> Enter a carriage return only when you wish to end a line and begin another, such as at the beginning of a new paragraph.

FIGURE 2-2   First Document, Forfun.

✔ CHECKPOINT

c.   Describe the purpose of the <CR> key in the WordPerfect program.

Position the cursor on the period at the end of the second paragraph then look at the status line.

d.   What is the current position number?

e.   What is the current line number?

SAVING DOCUMENTS

The document you have just typed is now stored in the computer's internal memory (primary storage). If you shut down the computer, your document will be lost.

In order to save your work, you must command the computer to place it on your data disk (secondary storage) in Drive B. Your newly created document will be added to the directory of files already stored on your WordPerfect Student Data disk.

NAMING DOCUMENTS

When you use the Save command, WordPerfect asks for a filename. The rules for naming files are explained in detail in Appendix A. A document is always stored and retrieved by the filename you give it. As your store of documents increases, it becomes more important to give each file a meaningful name. In time, you will develop your own system of naming files so that they can be quickly retrieved.

GUIDED ACTIVITY: SAVING A DOCUMENT

1. Press the F10 key.

    This prompt will appear in the status line: "Document to be Saved:"

2. Type "Forfun".

Document to be Saved: Forfun

FIGURE 2-3 Saving **Forfun.**

3. Press <CR>.

    The red light is now on for Drive B. This light indicates that your document is being saved on your WordPerfect Student Data disk in Drive B. While the computer is in the process of saving your document, the document remains on the screen just as you typed it. When the red light for Drive B shuts off, WordPerfect is ready for you to enter additional text.

✔ CHECKPOINT

    f. Identify the key that commands your computer to Save a document.

The Importance of Saving Documents

It happens sometimes that a power failure or inadvertent keystroke destroys data that has been stored in the computer's internal memory. This is a potential problem that is well worth your time and effort to avoid. Get into the habit of pausing every ten minutes to perform the Save function whenever you are working on a document.

Hint: Never remove a disk from a disk drive when the light is on; doing so may cause serious damage to either the disk or the computer.

THE CURSOR

The **cursor** is a flashing line that shows where the next typed character will appear on the computer display screen.   It appears in the top left corner of the screen each time you load the program.

CURSOR MOVEMENT KEYS

The cursor movement keys allow you to move the cursor easily to any position within your document.   These keys are located on the numeric keypad on the right side of your keyboard.   They consist of directional arrow keys, a home key, an end key, a page-up key, and a page-down key.

The cursor movement keys enable you to move the cursor to any position at which characters, numbers, or space have been keyed.   Therefore, if you wish to move beyond the end of your document (where nothing has been keyed), you must use <CR> instead of the cursor movement keys.

Horizontal Movement

The <Left> arrow key moves the cursor one character to the left each time it is pressed.   The <Right> arrow key moves the cursor one character to the right each time it is pressed.

When the <Left> and <Right> arrow keys are used in combination with the Ctrl key or immediately after the <Home> key, the cursor moves more quickly.   The Ctrl-<Right> arrow keys move the cursor one word to the right; the Ctrl-<Left> arrow keys move the cursor one word to the left.   The <Home>,<Right> arrow keys move the cursor to the right edge of the screen; the <Home>,<Left> arrow keys move the cursor to the left edge of the screen.   The <Home>,<Home>,<Right> arrow keys move the cursor to the right (end) of a line.   The <Home>,<Home>,<Left> arrow keys move the cursor to the left (beginning) of a line.

The <SPACEBAR> key moves the cursor one space to the right each time it is pressed.

Vertical Movement

The <Up> arrow key moves the cursor up one line on the document page.   The <Down> arrow key moves the cursor down one line on the document page.

When the <Up> and <Down> arrow keys are used in combination with the Ctrl key or immediately after the <Home> key, the cursor moves more quickly through the document. To move to the top or the bottom of the screen, press the <Home>,<Up> or <Home>,<Down> keys. To move to the top of the current page, press the Ctrl-<Home>,<Up> arrow keys; to move to the end of the current page, press the Ctrl-<Home>,<Down> arrow keys. To move to the beginning or the end of a document, press the <Home>,<Home>,<Up> arrow keys or the <Home>,<Home>,<Down> arrow keys.

Remember that the <CR> key ends one line and begins another. Therefore, if you press <CR> at the beginning of a line, you will insert a blank line into your document.

✔ CHECKPOINT

Use the vertical cursor movement keys to answer the following questions:

g. Move the cursor to the bottom left corner of the screen. What key or keys did you use?

_____

h. Move the cursor to the beginning of the document. What key or keys did you use?

_____

i. Move the cursor down two lines without creating blank lines. What key or keys on the numeric keypad did you use?

_____

How many times did you press the same key or keys?

_____

j. Move the cursor to the end of the document. What key or keys did you use? _____

k. Move the cursor up one line. What key or keys did you use?

_____

Use the horizontal cursor movement keys to answer the following questions:

l. Move the cursor one character to the right. What key or keys did you use? _____

m.   Move the cursor four words to the right. What key or keys did you use?

_____

How many times did you press the same key or keys?

_____

n.   Move the cursor to the right end of the line. What key or keys did you use? _____

o.   Move the cursor to the beginning of the line. What key or keys did you use? _____

Continue practicing with the cursor movement keys until you become proficient in moving the cursor through your document.

GO TO

The Go To keys, Ctrl-<Home>, move the cursor to a specific location in your document. The prompt "Go To" appears in the status line. Type a character after this prompt and the cursor will jump to the next occurrence of that character. Type a page number and the cursor will move to the beginning of the designated page.   Press the <Up> or <Down> arrow keys and the cursor will move to the beginning or end of the current page. Press the Block key and the cursor will move to the beginning of a highlighted block.

SAVING A DOCUMENT WHILE EXITING WORDPERFECT

When you are ready to end a working session, you can both Save and Exit WordPerfect with the same function key. You can Save and Exit from anywhere in a document; you need not move the cursor.

It is important to Exit WordPerfect correctly. Do not shut down the computer before pressing the Exit key.

GUIDED ACTIVITY: EXITING WORDPERFECT

1.   Press the F7 key.

This prompt will appear: "Save Document?(Y/N) Y"

The "Y" appears twice.   You can either type "Y" or press <CR> and the document will be saved. If you type "N", the document will not be saved.

2.   Type "Y".

This prompt will appear: "Document to be Saved: B:\FORFUN"

3.   Press <CR>.

This prompt will appear: "Replace B:\FORFUN (Y/N) N".

N is the default.

4.   Type "Y".

The document **Forfun** will be saved along with any revisions you have made. If you had typed "N", you would be prompted to enter a different filename. Your original document would still be stored in the original file, and your revised document would be stored in a new file with a new filename.

The red light is now on in Drive B, and the message "Saving B:\Forfun" appears on your screen.

After the file is saved, you will see this prompt: "Exit WP" (Y/N) N".   If you type "N" or press <CR>, a clear screen will appear. If you type "Y", WordPerfect will be exited and a DOS prompt will appear. When you see the DOS prompt, it is safe to remove the disks and shut down the computer.

5.   Type "N".

A clear screen will appear.

✔ CHECKPOINT

p.   Identify the key that both Saves your document and Exits WordPerfect.

q.   What does the prompt "Replace B:\FORFUN (Y/N)N" mean?

Hint: F1 is the Cancel key. It can be used to back out of WordPerfect features that display a message at the bottom of your screen, such as Exit, Retrieve, Block, and Search.   Therefore, if you change your mind after activating one of these features, just press F1.

THE HELP FUNCTION

WordPerfect allows you to access a Help screen anytime during your work on a document. Press F3 and a Help screen will appear. This screen lists, in alphabetical order, the features available in WordPerfect along with the name of the keys that activate each feature. You can also press any function key to get information about how that key is used. After you are finished browsing through the Help information, all you need do is press <CR> or <SPACEBAR> to return to the document on which you were working.

GUIDED ACTIVITY: USING THE HELP SCREEN

1. Remove your WordPerfect Student Data disk from Drive B and replace it with the WordPerfect Learning disk.

2. Press the F3 key.

   The following screen of instructions (Figure 2-4) will appear:

Help

   Press any letter to get an alphabetical list of features.

      The list will include the features that start with that letter, along with the name of the key where the feature is found. You can then press that key to get a description of how the feature works.

   Press any function key to get information about the use of the key.

      Some keys may let you choose from a menu to get more information about various options. Press HELP again to display the template.

   Press the Enter key or Spacebar to exit Help.

FIGURE 2-4   Help Screen Instructions.

3. Press the F10 key.

   The following screen of information on saving documents (Figure 2-5) will appear:

Save Text

The current document is saved on disk. The filename can have up to eight
characters, a period, followed by up to three more characters (_____.___).
If a file with that name already exists on disk, WordPerfect will ask you if
you wish to replace it.

Exit may also be used to save the document that you are working on. The only
difference is that the Save key returns you to your document.

FIGURE 2-5   Save (F10) Help Screen.

4. Press <CR> or <SPACEBAR> to exit Help.

RETRIEVING A DOCUMENT

When you end a working session and shut down your computer, the document that you
are working on does not remain in the computer's internal memory.   Remember,
though, that you have saved it on your data disk.   When you begin a new working
session, your first task will be to retrieve the document that you wish to edit.

GUIDED ACTIVITY: RETRIEVING A DOCUMENT

1. Press the Shift-F10 keys.

    This prompt will appear in the status line: "Document to be
    Retrieved:".

2. Type "Forfun".

Document to be Retrieved: Forfun

FIGURE 2-6 Retrieving Forfun.

3. Press <CR>.

    In a few seconds the document Forfun will appear on the screen.

✔   CHECKPOINT

    r.   Identify the keys that retrieve a stored document.

What You Have Accomplished

You have succeeded in retrieving the first document you created.   The Shift-F10 keys activate the Retrieve function.   When you typed "Forfun", you commanded your computer to look for your file, **Forfun**, on the disk in Drive B.

Hint: When you Retrieve a document, it appears on the screen at the cursor location.   You can Retrieve a document onto a clear screen or onto a screen that contains another document.   Unless you want to combine two documents into one file, make sure you have a clear screen before retrieving a document.

REVIEW QUESTIONS

1. Why should a separate drive be designated for saving files?

---

2. Identify the purpose of each element of the status line.

    a. _____

    b. _____

    c. _____

    d. _____

3. Which key activates the Save function?

---

4. Which cursor movement keys give you the fastest return to the beginning of your document?

---

5. How does pressing <SPACEBAR> change the cursor position?

---

6. Compare the purpose of the carriage return in a word-processing program with its purpose on a conventional typewriter.

---

7. Suppose that you are editing a document and wish to return to the beginning of the line you are editing. Which cursor movement key or keys should you use?

8. Which keys activate the Retrieve function?

9. Describe the procedure for saving a document.

10. Explain the importance of saving a document both during and at the end of each working session.

11. Explain the rules for naming files.

12. Suppose that you are editing a document and do not remember which keystrokes are needed to Save and Exit WordPerfect at the same time. What is the quickest way to find the needed information?

13. Describe how the cursor is used to guide you through the creation of a document.

14. Had you typed "For Fun" instead of "Forfun" when you named your document, under what filename would your document have been saved?

15. Which cursor movement keys provide the quickest movement down several pages?

DOCUMENTATION RESEARCH

1. Look up the description of "repeating keys" in the Getting Started section of your manual. Explain the meaning.

2.   In what two ways does WordPerfect refer to <CR> in the user's manual?

_____

3.   If you incorrectly type the name of a file you want to Retrieve, what message appears on the screen?

_____

4.   WordPerfect is **document oriented.**   Explain what this means.

_____

UNIT

3

TYPING AND PRINTING A BUSINESS LETTER

SUPPLIES NEEDED

1. WordPerfect program disk
2. WordPerfect Student Data disk
3. printer

OBJECTIVES

After completing this unit, you will be able to

1. correct typing errors by using specific delete keys;
2. identify and use specific toggle keys;
3. change from Insert to Typeover mode;
4. use the <TAB> key to indent;
5. insert additional text into a document;
6. print a document.

IMPORTANT KEYSTROKES

1. <TAB>..................to move cursor to the tab position
2. <BACKSPACE> key ....to delete one character to the left
3. <DEL> key..............to delete character the cursor is under
4. Ctrl-<BACKSPACE> keys..to delete one word
5. Ctrl-<End> keys........to delete to the end of a line (EOL)
6. Ctrl-<PgDn> keys.......to delete to the end of a page (EOP)
7. <INS> key..............to change from Insert to Typeover mode
8. Shift-F7...............to print a document
9. F1.....................to restore deleted text

ASSIGNMENTS

1. Create **Olson.ltr**
2. Edit **Olson.ltr**
3. Print **Olson.ltr**
4. Review Questions
5. Research Documentation

GUIDED ACTIVITY: CREATING A BUSINESS LETTER

Load WordPerfect. Remember to designate Drive B as your data storage drive. A clear screen will become the typing area on which you will type your second document.

1. Type "Ms. Sally Olson".

   A short line of text has been entered on Ln 1 of the screen.

2. Press <CR>.

   The cursor has moved to Ln 2, Pos 10, of your document.

3. Type "2469 Elm Street".

4. Press <CR>.

5. Type "Ourtown, MN 55642".

6. Press <CR>.

   Three short lines of text have now been created and appear on Ln 1-Ln 3 of the computer screen. The cursor is on Ln 4.

7. Press <CR> to create a blank line.

8. Type "Dear Ms. Olson:".

9. Press <CR> twice.

Ms. Sally Olson
2469 Elm Street
Ourtown, MN 55642

Dear Ms. Olson:

I am pleased to confirm January 15th as the delivery date for your new thirty-foot St. Croix Travel Trailer. The factory representatives assure me that the special options you ordered can be worked into their production schedule without any difficulty.

Our original quotation of $38,421 is now a firm price. It is payable at the time title is transferred.

We hope, Ms. Olson, you will return your trailer to us next fall so that we may winterize it. Our Service Department will do the following:

....wash and wax the outside
....check all electrical and mechanical features
....winterize the plumbing
....store the trailer on our premises

You have selected a fine travel trailer. I hope you will spend many enjoyable hours traveling.

Sincerely,

Robert Stand
President

Enclosure

FIGURE 3-1 Olson.ltr.

10. Type in the text of the letter shown in Figure 3-1.   At the end of a paragraph, press <CR> twice; once to end the paragraph and begin another and once to create a blank line between the two paragraphs.

Pause during the course of your work to save and name your file.   Name it "Olson.ltr".

11. Press <CR> twice to insert two blank lines before the closing.

12. Type "Sincerely,".

13. Press <CR> four times.

14. Type "Robert Stand".

15. Press <CR>.

16. Type "President".

17. Press <CR> two times.

18. Type "Enclosure".

After you have finished typing your letter, press F10 to Save it.

✔ CHECKPOINT

a. Which key is used to insert blank lines between paragraphs?

_____

b. When you come to the end of the letter and wish to insert a closing, how many times must you press <CR> to end the paragraph and insert two blank lines before the closing?

_____

EDITING A DOCUMENT

After creating a document, you need to proofread it for typing or spelling errors. You may also want to revise it by adding or deleting text. With WordPerfect, the tasks of proofreading and editing can be done right on the screen, thereby eliminating the need to retype an entire document.

GUIDED ACTIVITY: EDITING A BUSINESS LETTER

If the file Olson.ltr is not on your screen, press Shift-F10 to Retrieve it.

1. Move the cursor to the "t" in "15th" in the first line of the body of the letter.

2. Press <DEL> twice.

   The letters "t" and "h" have been deleted.

3. Leave the cursor where it is and type "t" and "h".

4. Now press <BACKSPACE> twice.

   The letters "t" and "h" have again been deleted.

5. Move the cursor to the letter "l" in the word "travel" in the first line of the last paragraph.

6. Press the Ctrl-<BACKSPACE> keys.   (These are combination keys, so hold down the Ctrl key while you press <BACKSPACE>.)

   The word "travel" has been deleted.

7. Move the cursor to the "E" in the word "Enclosure" at the end of the letter.

8. Press the Ctrl-<End> keys.

   The entire line (in this case the line consists of only one word) has been deleted.

✔ CHECKPOINT

   c. If your cursor is positioned directly on a character that you wish to delete, which key must you press?

_____

   d. Which keys will most quickly accomplish the task of deleting an entire line?

_____

TOGGLE KEYS

When you press a key to turn a specific command on and then press it again to turn it off, you are using a **toggle key**. WordPerfect assigns a number of commands to toggle keys. This is a convenient way to use the keyboard, for, as you become familiar with specific commands and the keyboard, toggling becomes as easy as turning a light switch on and off.

The Insert Key

If you press the <INS> (insert) key on your keyboard, you switch to the Typeover mode. In the Typeover mode the character on which the cursor is located is replaced by the character you are typing. The prompt "Typeover" appears on the status line. This is an alternative to using the delete keys to erase existing text.

Simply press <INS> again to toggle off the Typeover mode and return to Insert mode.

THE REWRITE FEATURE

You may notice that when you insert additional text in the middle of a line, the words at the right edge of the screen seem to disappear. By simply pressing any cursor movement key, you can make these words reappear in the proper format. This is WordPerfect's Rewrite feature; it moves existing text over to make room for the text you are adding. Whenever you edit text, either by inserting or deleting, the text on the screen is rewritten.

GUIDED ACTIVITY: USING THE <TAB> AND <INS> KEYS

The tabs in WordPerfect have been preset to every five spaces. Therefore, when you wish to indent a paragraph, simply press <TAB>.

1. Retrieve **Olson.ltr** if necessary.

2. Move the cursor to the letter "I", which is the first word of the first paragraph.

3. Press <TAB>.

    The first line of the first paragraph is now indented five spaces. The cursor is in Pos 15. Move the cursor with any directional arrow key and the paragraph will be rewritten.

4. Use the <TAB> key to indent the first line of each paragraph in your letter to Ms. Olson.

5. Move the cursor to the space between "15" and "as" in the first line of the first paragraph.

6. Type "," (comma).

7. Press <SPACEBAR>.

8. Type "1987,".

   The year has been inserted into the text.

9. Move the cursor to the "3" in the price, "$38,421".

10. Press <INS> to toggle on the Typeover feature.

    The prompt "Typeover" will appear at the bottom of the screen.

11. Type "37,982".

    The price has been replaced with new figures.

12. Press <INS> to toggle off the Typeover feature.

    The prompt "Typeover" has disappeared from the bottom of the screen.

13. Press the F10 key to Save the revised letter.

✔   CHECKPOINT

e. What column position will your cursor be in if you press <TAB> three times?

GUIDED ACTIVITY: PRINTING A BUSINESS LETTER

1. Retrieve **Olson.ltr** if necessary.

   When the letter appears on your screen, you are ready to Print.

2. Press Shift-F7.

   A Print menu (Figure 3-2) will appear at the bottom of the screen. This menu provides you with several options for printing your document. The Print menu is discussed in detail in Unit 7. For now, you will print the full text of your business letter so that you can see a **hard copy** (printed output) of **Olson.ltr**.

```
1 Full Text; 2 Page; 3 Change Options; 4 Printer Control; 5 Type-thru: 0
```

FIGURE 3-2   Print Menu.

Make sure that the printer you are using is supplied with paper, and that the power, ready, and on line lights are on. If you need guidance, check with your instructor.

3. Type "1".

A "Please wait" prompt will appear at the bottom of your screen, and in a few seconds the printer will begin to print your document.

You now have a copy of the business letter you typed, and it is ready to be mailed.

4. Press F7 to Exit WordPerfect.

✔ CHECKPOINT

f. List the three steps required to print the full text of a document.

_____

UNDELETE

WordPerfect saves up to three deletions. To retrieve deleted text, move the cursor to the location you want the text restored and press F1. The Undelete menu appears on the screen. The text you last deleted is highlighted at the cursor location. Select Option 1 to restore the highlighted text. Select Option 2 and use the <Up> and <Down> arrow keys to find a previous deletion; then select Option 1 to restore it.

REVIEW QUESTIONS

1. A standard business letter requires two line spaces between the salutation and the text. Which key provides these two blank lines?

_____

2. Identify the keys that Retrieve a document.

_____

3. If you want to print the full text of a document, which option from the Print menu should you choose?

_____

4. You prefer typing over existing text, rather than using delete keys, to make changes. How do you switch from Insert to Typeover mode?

_____

5. Define "toggle."

_____

6. When you insert text within a document, existing text sometimes appears to run off the edge of the screen. Why does this occur?

_____

7. Which key Saves a document.

_____

8. Holding down the delete key deletes all characters from the cursor to the right margin. Which keys delete such characters more efficiently.

_____

9. Suppose that in revising a document you discover that the information on a given page is no longer correct. How can you quickly delete the entire page?

_____

10. List the steps required to edit the following line:

    "All the world's a staage and all the men and women players."

    a. Identify the cursor position and keystroke required to delete the extra "a" in "stage".

_____

    b. How would you insert "merely" between the words "women" and "players"?

_____

11. Which key would you use to indent five spaces?

_____

DOCUMENTATION RESEARCH

1. Describe how the <ESC> key can be used with the delete EOL keys to delete several lines at a time.

_____

2. WordPerfect saves your last three deletions in case you decide to restore them. What message appears on the screen when the program has run out of room to store deleted text?

_____

3. List some reasons why WordPerfect might generate an error message.

_____

4. Look up Cancel in the Reference section. List each function this key can cancel.

_____

APPLICATION

SUPPLIES NEEDED

1. WordPerfect program disk
2. WordPerfect Student Data disk
3. WordPerfect Learning disk
4. printer

ASSIGNMENTS

The assignments to be completed for this Application section are

1. Create Apply.ltr
2. Create Reserve.ltr
3. Create Newspapr.ltr

APPLICATIONS

This Application section contains a number of documents that can be reproduced to apply the skills you have acquired in Units 1 through 3. Format your documents so that they look like the ones on the printed pages of this section. Some format instructions have been handwritten on the pages of this section to guide you. Remember that right justification does not appear on the screen; it appears when a document is printed.

Use your template and the Quick Reference card to find the keystroke commands and menus you need. Remember that there is often more than one keystroke choice that can be used to create and format a document. Your primary task is to find the most efficient way to reproduce the documents.

You may also want to create your own applications--some tasks that are more meaningful to your everyday work. Your WordPerfect Student Data disk should have plenty of space available to store additional documents.

3740 Johnson Drive
Denton, Minnesota 55802
March 6, 1987

Mr. John Holmes
Manager, Benton Park
3789 Lonesome Trail
Barton, Michigan 55660

Dear Mr. Holmes:

I am responding to your advertisement for an office assistant in the Barton Chronicle. I wish to apply for this position.

I am a business major at Lakeview Community College, Denton, Minnesota. I have completed financial and managerial accounting courses as well as several general business courses. I am presently working as a student assistant in the school library.

I am enclosing my resume and two letters of recommendation. I am available for an interview on any weekend or during spring break, which begins on March 13 and ends on March 22. My telephone number is (612) 422-1234.

Sincerely yours,

William Johnson

Enclosures

Name this document Apply.ltr

3740 Johnson Drive
Denton, Minnesota 55802
April 4, 1987

Ms. Mary Neuman, Manager
LONE PINE MOTEL
4007 Blue Spruce Street
Barton, Michigan 55660

Dear Ms. Neuman,

I would like to reserve a single room on April 28 and April 29,
1987.   I am arriving at the Barton International Airport at
9:30 p.m.   Please hold my room reservation for me.

I am enclosing a check for the $25.00 advance reservation fee.
Please confirm my reservation as soon as possible.

Sincerely yours,

William Johnson

Enclosure

Name this document Reserve.ltr

3740 Johnson Drive
Denton, Minnesota 55802
May 15, 1987

Circulation Department
Minnesota Dispatch
456 9th Street
St. Paul, Minnesota 55104

Dear Sir:

From June 1, 1987, through August 25, 1987, I would like my
newspaper mailed to the following address:

Mr. William Johnson
Assistant Manager, Benton Park
3789 Lonesome Trail
Barton, Michigan 55660

I am enclosing a check that covers the three-month subscription
cost as well as the postage.

Yours truly,

William Johnson
Assistant Manager

Enclosure

Name this document Newspapr.ltr

UNIT

4 SIMPLE EDITING FUNCTIONS

SUPPLIES NEEDED

1. WordPerfect program disk
2. two WordPerfect Student Data disks
3. printer

OBJECTIVES

After completing this unit, you will be able to

1. center text;
2. underline and boldface text;
3. revise multiple lines of text by using the Block feature;
4. insert text at the right margin;
5. move a block of text;
6. convert a block of text from upper- to lower-case and from lower- to upper-case letters;
7. reveal codes.

43

IMPORTANT KEYSTROKES

1. F6......................to boldface text
2. F8......................to underline text
3. <CAPS LOCK>.............to capitalize text
4. Shift-F6................to center text horizontally
5. Alt-F6..................to begin a Flush Right
6. Alt-F4..................to define a block of text
7. Ctrl-F4.................to move or copy a block of text
8. Shift-F3................to convert a block of text from upper- to lower-
                            case and from lower- to upper-case letters
9. Alt-F3..................to reveal codes

ASSIGNMENTS

1. Revise **Olson.ltr**
2. Print **Olson.ltr** (Revised)
3. Review Questions
4. Research Documentation

ENHANCEMENT FEATURES

You have discovered how WordPerfect lets you easily manipulate text to create a simple business report or letter. WordPerfect also provides a number of features that can enhance text to make a printed copy look more attractive and professional.

The Bold Feature

Boldface text is darker than normal and is commonly used for titles and headers. A single keystroke embeds a code that instructs the printer to double-strike specified characters.

The Underline Feature

Some words and phrases, such as book and magazine titles, require underlining. You may also wish to underline portions of text for emphasis. Again, a single keystroke embeds a code that instructs the printer to underline specified characters.

Capitalization

At times you may wish to capitalize an entire string of letters. By toggling on the <CAPS LOCK> key, you can capitalize without holding down the Shift key. The

<CAPS LOCK> key affects only alphabetic characters, not numbers or punctuation marks as on a conventional typewriter.

When the <CAPS LOCK> key is on, holding down the Shift key results in producing lower-case letters.

Centering Text

Headers and titles are often centered, either on a page or over a column. When you press the Center key, text is automatically centered around the position you select.

Hint: You can always tell when you have activated one of these enhancement features, because they are revealed on the screen. When the <CAPS LOCK> key is toggled on, POS in the status line appears in upper-case letters. When either the Underline or Bold feature is toggled on, the position number in the status line and the text appear in a contrasting color or intensity. The underline does not appear on all screens, but it will appear on your printed document. If you press Center when your cursor is at the left margin, the line of text is centered on the screen.

GUIDED ACTIVITY: CREATING A LETTERHEAD

1. Use Shift-F10 to Retrieve **Olson.ltr**.

2. Position your cursor on Ln 1, Pos 10, of the document.

3. Press <CR> twice.

    The text of **Olson.ltr** has been moved down two lines. Two blank lines have been created at the top of the page.

4. Use the cursor movement keys to move the cursor back to Ln 1, Pos 10.

5. Press the <CAPS LOCK> key.

6. Press the Shift-F6 keys to activate the Center function.

7. Press the F6 key to activate the Bold function.

8. Press the F8 key to activate the Underline function.

9. Type "st. croix travel trailer company".

    The typed phrase will be centered, capitalized, boldface, and underlined.

10.   Press <CR>.

The cursor has jumped to Ln 2, Pos 10, of your document.   Pressing <CR> terminated the Center function.

11.   Press the F8 key to toggle off the Underline function.

12.   Press the <CAPS LOCK> key to toggle back to lower-case letters.

13.   Press the Shift-F6 keys to Center.

14.   Type "415 Smith Street".

(With the <CAPS LOCK> key off, you must again use the Shift key to capitalize letters.)

15.   Press <CR>.

The cursor has jumped to Ln 3, Pos 10, of your document.

16.   Press the Shift-F6 keys to activate the Center function.

17.   Type "St. Paul, MN   55108".

18.   Press <CR> four times.

The cursor has moved to Ln 7, Pos 10.

19.   Press the F6 key to toggle off the Bold function.

What You Have Accomplished

You have enhanced your business letter by adding a letterhead.   You have learned the keystrokes that activate commands that allow you to capitalize letters without using the Shift key, to center a line of text horizontally, to underline specific words or phrases, and to create boldface type.   You have also learned that the <CAPS LOCK> key, the F6 (Bold) key, and the F8 (Underline) key are toggle keys.

✔ CHECKPOINT

a.   How does the status line change when you toggle on the Bold function?

_____

b.   Which toggle key underlines text?

_____

c. Which toggle key creates boldface text?

_____

d. Which toggle key capitalizes alphabetic characters?

_____

e. Which keys Center text horizontally?

_____

f. How can you terminate the Center feature?

_____

Hint: You toggle a key (F6) to turn Bold on, then toggle F6 again to turn Bold off.   Each time you toggle the key, a different code is embedded. Now you can insert text anywhere in the word or phrase that you boldface and it will be boldface as well.   This is also true of the Underline function but does not apply to <CAPS LOCK>.   The Center command terminates each time you press <CR> and is not activated again until you press Shift-F6.

THE FLUSH RIGHT FEATURE

Text is usually entered from the left and aligned precisely against the left margin.   There are times, however, when you might prefer to enter text from the right and align it against the right margin.   After you activate the Flush Right function, all text that you enter moves across the screen from right to left (rather than the usual left to right) and aligns flush against the right margin. This feature is often used to enter dates or business headings.

GUIDED ACTIVITY: INSERTING THE CURRENT DATE FLUSH RIGHT

Your document, Olson.ltr, should be on the screen.   Make sure that you are in Insert mode and that your cursor is positioned on Ln 7, Pos 10.

1. Press Alt-F6.

    The cursor will align itself along the edge of the right margin.

2. Type the current date.

    Text will be entered from right to left.

3.   Press <CR>.

The Flush Right feature has been terminated.

✔ CHECKPOINT

g.   What happened to the cursor when you pressed Alt-F6?

_____

THE BLOCK FEATURE

The Block feature is an efficient way to revise multiple lines of text. The Block key (Alt-F4), used in combination with other command keys, can quickly and efficiently make the changes you desire.

When you toggle on Block, a "Block on" message appears on the screen. Use the cursor movement keys to highlight the portion (block) of text you wish to revise.

GUIDED ACTIVITY: USING THE BLOCK FEATURE TO ENHANCE EXISTING TEXT

1.   Move the cursor to the first letter of the word "St." in the first paragraph of **Olson.ltr.**

2.   Press the Alt-F4 keys.

The Block feature has been turned on. A flashing message, "Block on", will appear in the status line.

3.   Move the cursor across the words "St. Croix Travel Trailer".

The cursor has highlighted the block of text you wish to revise.

4.   Press the F6 key.

The highlighted text will appear in boldface. Pressing F6 also automatically turned off the Block and Bold functions. Notice that the boldface text on your screen contrasts with normal text.

✔ CHECKPOINT

h.   Which keys are used to define the area of text that is to be boldface?

_____

5. Move the cursor to the first letter of the word "fine" in the last paragraph of your letter.

6. Press the Alt-F4 keys.

    The Block feature has been turned on again.

7. Move the cursor across the word "fine" to highlight it.

8. Press the F8 key.

    The highlighted text has been underlined. The Block and Underline features have been turned off.

9. Move the cursor to the first letter of the word "firm" in the second paragraph.

10. Press the Alt-F4 keys.

    The Block feature has been turned on again.

11. Highlight the word "firm".

12. Press the F6 key.

    The highlighted text has been boldfaced. The Block and Bold features have been turned off.

13. Make sure the cursor is on the first letter of the word "firm".

14. Press the Alt-F4 keys.

    The Block feature has been turned on again.

15. Highlight the word "firm".

16. Press the F8 key.

    The highlighted text is underlined. The Block and Underline features have been turned off.

✔ CHECKPOINT

    i. How does the screen display change when you press F6?

    _____

    j. How does the screen display change when you press F8?

    _____

Hint: If you change your mind and decide not to revise text after you have blocked it, press the Alt-F4 keys to turn off the Block feature. The Cancel key (F1) also turns off the Block feature. F1 is not a toggle key. It is a key assigned to cancel specific functions, such as turning off the Block feature.

What You Have Accomplished

You have used the Block key in combination with other function keys to revise blocks of text. You have discovered that the Block feature is an efficient way to alter the appearance of a document with a minimum number of keystrokes.

MENU

A menu is a list of choices available to the user of a software program. Menu selections are usually made with a keyboard entry. Menus simplify operations, save time, and reduce data entry errors.

THE MOVE AND COPY FEATURES

One of your most basic editing functions is to copy and move text. When you move a block of text, you remove it from its original location and place it in a new location in your document. When you copy a block of text, you place it in an additional location in your document.

The Move and Copy features are used in combination with the Block feature. Press the Alt-F4 keys (to turn on the Block feature); move your cursor to highlight a block of text, and press the Ctrl-F4 keys. The Move menu (Figure 4-1) will appear in the status line.

Options 1 and 2 on this menu are used to move and copy text.

1 Cut Block; 2 Copy Block; 3 Append; 4 Cut/Copy Column; 5 Cut/Copy Rectangle: 0

FIGURE 4-1 Move Menu (Block On).

The first two options on this menu are defined as follows:

  1 Cut Block. This option is used to Move blocks of text. The highlighted (blocked) text disappears from the screen. It reappears at the cursor location when Ctrl-F4 is pressed again.

2 Copy Block. This option is used to Copy blocks of text. The highlighted text does not disappear from the screen. It is copied at the cursor location when Ctrl-F4 is pressed.

After selecting one of these two options, move the cursor to the highlighted text you wish to Move or Copy; then press Ctrl-F4. The Move and Retrieve menu (Figure 4-2) will appear on your screen. Type "5" to retrieve the text you have copied or cut. The highlighted block of text will reappear.

Move 1 Sentence; 2 Paragraph; 3 Page; Retrieve 4 Column; 5 Text; 6 Rectangle: 0

FIGURE 4-2 Move and Retrieve Menu.

GUIDED ACTIVITY: MOVING A BLOCK OF TEXT

1. Move the cursor to the first bullet in front of the "w" in the word "wash" in the list of services in **Olson.ltr.**

2. Press the Alt-F4 keys to turn on the Block feature.

3. Highlight the line.

4. Press the Ctrl-F4 keys.

    The Move menu will appear at the bottom of the screen.

5. Type "1".

    The line of text will disappear from the screen.

6. Move the cursor to the first bullet in front of the "s" in the word "store", the last item of the list.

7. Press <CR> to insert a blank line.

8. Move the cursor to Pos 10 on the blank line you just created.

9. Press the Ctrl-F4 keys.

    The Move and Retrieve menu will appear at the bottom of the screen.

10. Type "5" .

    The line of text will reappear at your cursor location.

11.   Delete the blank line at the beginning of the list with the <DEL> key.

✔   CHECKPOINT

   k.   List the six steps needed to move a block of text.

_____

APPEND TO FILE

This feature lets you add a block of text to an existing file.   First, Block the text you wish to append; then press Ctrl-F4 to access the Move menu.   Select option 3 from the Move menu.   You will be prompted to enter the name of the file you wish to append.

THE BLOCK AND SWITCH FUNCTIONS

After typing a document, you may decide to revise an entire paragraph by using all upper-case letters; or you may type a paragraph entirely in capital letters and then change your mind.   The Block and Switch features let you make these changes quickly.

You can use the Block (Alt-F4) and Switch (Shift-F3) features to convert a block of text to all upper-case or all lower-case letters.   First highlight the text you wish to convert, then turn on the Switch feature.   The Block and Switch menu (Figure 4-3) allows you to choose either upper- or lower-case letters.

```
Block 1 Upper Case; 2 Lower Case: 0
```

FIGURE 4-3   Block and Switch Menu.

GUIDED ACTIVITY: USING THE BLOCK AND SWITCH FEATURES

1.   Move the cursor two lines below the word "President" at the end of Olson.ltr.

2.   Type "P.S.   Thank you for doing business with us."

3.   Move the cursor to the "h" in the word "Thank".

4.   Press Alt-F4 to turn on Block.

5.   Move the cursor to highlight the rest of the postscript.

6. Press the Shift-F3 keys.

    The Block and Switch menu will appear at the bottom of your screen.

7. Type "1".

    The highlighted letters will change from lower- to upper-case.

8. Press the Alt-F4 keys.

    The Block feature has been turned off.

9. Move the cursor to the last "." (period) in "P.S.".

10. Press Alt-F4 to turn on Block.

11. Highlight the rest of the postscript.

12. Press Shift-F3 to turn on Switch.

13. Type "2".

    You have chosen to convert the character string in the postscript from upper- to lower-case letters. Because you highlighted the period from the preceding sentence, the first letter of the postscript remains a capitalized letter. This is the most efficient way to convert a block of text from upper- to lower-case letters while still retaining the initial capital letter.

14. Press Alt-F4 to turn off Block.

✔ CHECKPOINT

    l. Identify the keys that turn the Block and Switch features on.

    _____

    m. How can you convert an entire paragraph from upper- to lower-case letters and still retain an initial capital letter?

    _____

Hint: You have noticed by now that the same editing function can sometimes be accomplished with different keystroke commands. By choosing the right alternative, you can reduce the total number of keystrokes you must make. The keystrokes you choose are also determined by the task you are performing with WordPerfect. For example, the way you manipulate text in a long report or proposal differs from the way you manipulate text in a form letter.

GUIDED ACTIVITY: PRINTING A REVISED BUSINESS LETTER

Your revised business letter is ready to be printed.

1.   Press Shift-F7 to access the Print menu.

2.   Type "1".

     A "Please wait" message will appear in the status line, then your document
     will be printed.

3.   Press F7 to Exit WordPerfect.

The revised **Olson.ltr** should look like that in Figure 4-4.

What You Have Accomplished

You have revised **Olson.ltr**. The text of your letter is both left- and right-
justified, which means that the first character of each line is aligned precisely
against the left margin and the last character of each line is aligned precisely
against the right margin. Right justification was not shown on the screen but
appears in the printed document.

REVEAL CODES

The text on your screen appears in much the same format as your printed document.
You can see boldfacing and underlining, indented paragraphs, double spacing, and
so forth. All of the codes you have embedded are, however, invisible.

At times it is helpful to see the codes that have been placed in your document—to
track down, for example, the cause of a printing or print-formatting problem. The
Reveal Codes feature helps you in such a situation.

When you press the Alt-F3 keys, the screen is split in two by the Tab Ruler. The
upper window displays normal text; the lower window displays the text along with
the hidden codes. The cursor appears as a blinking "^" in the lower window. Each
window displays three lines of text above the blinking cursor.

The cursor movement keys move you simultaneously through the text of each window.
A limited amount of editing can be done with the <BACKSPACE>, or <DEL> keys. Any
other key returns you to the normal screen.

ST. CROIX TRAVEL TRAILER COMPANY
415 Smith Street
St. Paul, MN 55108

(Today's date)

Ms. Sally Olson
2469 Elm Street
Ourtown, MN 55642

Dear Ms. Olson:

I am pleased to confirm January 15, 1987, as the delivery date for your new thirty-foot **St. Croix Travel Trailer**. The factory representatives assure me that the special options you ordered can be worked into their production schedule without any difficulty.

Our original quotation of $37,982 is now a <u>firm</u> price. It is payable at the time title is transferred.

We hope, Ms. Olson, you will return your trailer to us next fall so that we may winterize it. Our Service Department will do the following:

....check all electrical and mechanical features
....winterize the plumbing
....wash and wax the outside
....store the trailer on our premises

You have selected a <u>fine</u> travel trailer. I hope you will spend many enjoyable hours traveling.

Sincerely,

Robert Stand
President

P.S. Thank you for doing business with us.

FIGURE 4-4 **Olson.ltr** (Revised).

GUIDED ACTIVITY: REVEALING CODES

1. Retrieve Olson.ltr.

2. Press Alt-F3.

    The Tab Ruler has split the screen. Several lines of text appear above the
    Tab Ruler; the same text with codes embedded appears below the ruler.

✔ CHECKPOINT

    n. Which keystrokes are needed to activate the Reveal Codes feature?

_____

3. Move the cursor in the upper window until it reaches the first line of the
    heading.

✔ CHECKPOINT

    o. What two codes are embedded in front of the first line of the heading to
    indicate that the first line of the heading is centered and underlined?

_____

4. Move the cursor in the upper window until it reaches the date line.

✔ CHECKPOINT

    p. What codes in the date line indicate that the Flush Right function was
    used?

_____

5. Move the cursor in the upper window until it reaches the last paragraph of
    the body of the letter.

✔ CHECKPOINT

    q. What codes indicate that the word "firm" is both underlined and
    boldfaced?

_____

6. Move the cursor through the document as you examine the codes. Notice that the settings on the Tab Ruler reflect the margin and tab settings.

MAKING BACKUP COPIES OF YOUR DOCUMENTS

You have already learned to manage the potential loss of data by frequently using the Save function (F10). Another way to protect your data is by making backup copies. As new documents are created, copy them onto your second WordPerfect Student Data disk. Then, if your original copy is physically damaged or the files inadvertently erased, you still have a copy of your documents.

Refer to the Copy section of Appendix A, to learn how to make backup copies of your documents.

REVIEW QUESTIONS

1. The cursor movement keys are important in using the Block feature to edit text. Explain how these keys are used.

2. The date in a business letter is usually placed flush right. How do you place text flush right in a document?

3. Explain how the Block feature is used.

4. Describe the process of converting an entire block of text from upper- to lower-case letters.

5. How would you go about centering text to create a letterhead in a business letter?

6. Which toggle key creates boldface type?

7. How do you turn off the Underline feature?

8. How does the screen change to let you know that the Bold function is turned on? How does it change to let you know that the Underline function is on?

_____

9. The Block and Switch features convert a block of text to all upper- or all lower-case letters. Describe how the text changes when you highlight the mark from the preceding sentence before you turn the Switch feature on.

_____

10. What command is needed to transfer a copy of a file from a disk in Drive A to a disk in Drive B?

_____

11. Suppose that you type a business letter and then decide to place your last paragraph first. What keys are needed to rearrange your text?

_____

12. Suppose that your document is not printing out in the format you expect. How would you investigate your printing problem?

_____

DOCUMENTATION RESEARCH

1. It may happen that in revising a boldface title you move the delete key across the code to boldface. How does the program respond when this happens?

_____

2. List some of the features that can be used in combination with the Block key.

_____

3. Which keys are needed to use the Block feature in combination with more than one other feature at a time?

_____

4. Where should the cursor be placed when you are using the Block feature with the Flush Right feature?

_____

5. The Block and Switch keys can be used together to convert text to upper- or lower-case letters. In what other way can the Switch feature be used?

_____

6. Assume that you have finished the first chapter of your new book. There are several paragraphs in your manuscript that you would like to set aside for use in a later chapter. Explain how this can be done.

_____

7. What do the codes [SRt] and [HRt] mean?

_____

8. List the codes that are embedded in your document when you issue the following commands.

   a. Center Text_____

   b. Block_____

   c. Bold_____

   d. Flush Right_____

   e. Headers or Footers_____

   f. Double Indent_____

   g. Justification On_____

   h. Hard Page_____

9. Name two ways to delete codes that you have entered incorrectly.

_____

5 FORMATTING TEXT FOR PRINTING

SUPPLIES NEEDED

1. WordPerfect program disk
2. WordPerfect Student Data disk
3. printer

OBJECTIVES

After completing this unit, you will be able to

1. use the Print Format menu to format a printed page;
2. use the Line Format menu to set tab stops, margins, and line spacing;
3. use the Page Format menu to number document pages;
4. use the Print menu to choose options for printing.

IMPORTANT KEYSTROKES

1. Ctrl-F8............................to format for printing
2. Shift-F8...........................to format a line
3. Alt F8.............................to format a page
4. Shift-F7...........................to print
5. Shift-<TAB>........................to move one tab stop to the left

FORMATTING TEXT FOR PRINTING

You have discovered a number of editing functions that will make your documents attractive and your word-processing tasks easier.

Your documents must also be formatted. Whereas editing affects the appearance and content of the text, formatting affects the appearance of the document on the printed page. When you prepare a document for printing you must set margins and tabs, specify the number of spaces between lines (e.g., single, double, or triple spacing), and determine a pattern for numbering pages. With some documents you must also set headers and footers, determine column widths, or adjust the justification parameters.

Some of the formatting options WordPerfect offers are dependent on the printer that interfaces with the computer you are using. Some printers allow you to embed a code that commands the printer to change the pitch (type size) or type style during the course of printing. There are also specialized typing functions available with WordPerfect that can be used only with a compatible printer. These special features include overstrikes for diacritical marks in foreign words, superscripts, subscripts, and mathematical formulas.

In Unit 5, we focus on formatting text for printing. The unit is divided into three sections to help differentiate between each Print Format function and to make the working sessions manageable. Unit 6 guides you through the steps required to control your printer.

SECTION 1

ASSIGNMENTS

1. Create Quote.txt
2. Review Questions
3. Research Documentation

THE PRINT FORMAT KEY

The Print Format key is F8.   When you place your template over the function keypad, you see the word "FORMAT" printed vertically next to the words "print," "line," and "page."   Notice that Ctrl-F8, Shift-F8 and Alt-F8 are the function keys used to format.

Whenever any one of these key combinations is pressed, a menu of choices is displayed.   Choosing an option from a menu embeds a code in your document that the processor in turn sends to the printer.

THE PRINT FORMAT MENU

When the Ctrl-F8 keys are pressed, the Print Format menu appears on your screen (Figure 5-1).   This menu offers you several options for formatting text.   You may select an option by typing one of the listed numbers.

```
Print Format

    1 - Pitch                          10
        Font                            1

    2 - Lines per Inch                  6

    Right Justification                On
    3 - Turn off                        .
    4 - Turn on

    Underline Style                     5
        5 - Non-continuous Single
        6 - Non-continuous Double
        7 - Continuous Single
        8 - Continuous Double

    9 - Sheet Feeder Bin Number         1

    A - Insert Printer Command


Selection:   0
```

FIGURE 5-1 Print Format Menu.

The Print Format menu options are defined as follows:

1 Pitch.   Pitch refers to the size of type which affects the number of characters per horizontal inch. The default is 10 (ten characters per inch) and is called **pica** type. Another commonly used type is *elite* type, which prints twelve characters per horizontal inch.

If you type an asterisk after the pitch number (10*), your printed copy will contain proportional spacing; that is, the printer will distinguish between the width of individual characters. Since character widths vary, the number of characters that fit on a line also varies. When you change pitch it is also necessary to change margins settings.

NOT ALL PRINTERS SUPPORT PITCH CHANGES OR PROPORTIONAL SPACING.

Font. Font refers to type style. It is preset to 1.

2 Lines per Inch. When the default is chosen, a document is printed with six vertical lines per inch.

Right Justification

3 Turn off. A document is printed with an even left margin and an uneven right margin.

4 Turn on. The spacing between printed characters is automatically adjusted so that a document is printed with an even right margin as well as an even left margin.

The default is set for Justification On.

Underline Style. This option allows you to choose a style for underlining text as you type it.

5 Non-continuous Single. This style does not underline tabs. It does underline spaces. A document is printed with one-line underlining.

6 Non-continuous Double. This style underlines spaces but not tabs. A document is printed with two-line underlining.

7 Continuous Single. This style underlines tabs and spaces. A printed document contains a single underline.

8 Continuous Double. This style underlines tabs and spaces. A printed document contains a double underline.

9 Sheet Feeder Bin Number. If your printer provides more than one bin, this option allows you to send specific parts of a document to different bins, The default for this option is bin 1.

A Insert Printer Command. This option allows you to send any command that your printer recognizes.

Hint: It takes some time and patience to learn how specific print format commands affect your printed document. Do some experimenting until you find the styles that suit you and that your printer can accommodate. Always think through the commands you embed in a document, because the printer follows instructions exactly as they are given.

GUIDED ACTIVITY: COPYING A BLOCK OF TEXT

1. Display a clear screen.

2. Type the text in Figure 5-2.

If you treat a man as he is, you make him worse than he is. If you treat him as if he already were what he potentially could be, you make him what he should be.   Goethe

FIGURE 5-2 **Quote.txt.**

3. Press <CR> after the name "Goethe".

4. Move the cursor to Ln 1, Pos 10.

5. Press the Alt-F4 keys to turn on the Block function.

6. Highlight the entire quotation by moving the cursor to the end of the paragraph.

7. Press the Ctrl-F4 keys.

    The Move menu will appear on the screen.

8. Type "2" to choose Copy.

    Your text is no longer highlighted (Block is now off).

9. Press <CR> four times.

10. Press the Ctrl-F4 keys.

    The Move and Retrieve menu will appear on the screen.

11.   Type "5" to choose Text.

      The quotation will be copied at the cursor location.

12.   Move the cursor to the blank line after the copied quotation.

13.   Press <CR> four times.

14.   Copy the quotation two more times (a total of four copies of the quotation) by redoing steps 11 through 13.

15.   Move the cursor to the second line below the first quotation.

16.   Type "The above quotation is in 10 pitch".

17.   Save this document with the filename "Quote.txt".

GUIDED ACTIVITY: CHANGING THE PITCH

1.   Move the cursor to the first letter of the second quotation.

2.   Press the Ctrl-F8 keys.

      The Print Format menu will appear on the screen.

3.   Type "1".

      The 0 (zero) after the word "Selection" will be replaced by a 1. The cursor is now located on the "10" next to the word "Pitch".

4.   Type "12".

      The default has been overridden and your document will be printed in elite type (twelve characters per horizontal inch).

5.   Press <CR> three times.

      Your document will reappear on the screen.

6.   Move the cursor to the second line below the second quotation.

7.   Type "The above quotation is in 12 pitch.".

8.   Move the cursor to the next blank line.

9.   Press the Ctrl-F8 keys.

      The Print Format menu will again appear on the screen.

10. Type "1" to select Pitch.

Pitch has been selected.

11. Type "10".

The pitch has been changed back to the default setting of 10.

12. Press <CR> three times.

Your document will reappear on the screen.

What You Have Accomplished

You used the Block key and the Move menu to copy a block of text three times. You then used the Ctrl-F8 keys to access the Print Format menu and change the pitch of one of the copied quotations from 10 (the default setting) to 12 (elite type).

When you change pitch, you must also change margin settings. This is done in another Guided Activity. Keep in mind that not all printers support pitch changes. Therefore it is also necessary that you become familiar with your printer's capabilities before using the options on the Print Format menu.

✔ CHECKPOINT

a. What menu appears when the Ctrl-F8 keys are pressed?

===

b. What number must you type to set the pitch to elite?

===

GUIDED ACTIVITY: RIGHT JUSTIFICATION

1. Retrieve Quote.txt if necessary.

2. Move the cursor to the first letter of the third copy of the quotation.

3. Press the Ctrl-F8 keys.

The Print Format menu will appear on the screen.

4. Type "3".

Right justification has been turned off. The word "On" has changed to the word "Off."   The third copy of the quotation will be printed with an even left margin and an uneven right margin.

5. Press the <CR> key.

    Your document will reappear on the screen.

6. Move the cursor to the second blank line following the third copy of the quotation.

7. Type "The above quotation is left-justified only.".

8. Move the cursor to the next blank line.

9. Press the Ctrl-F8 keys.

    The Print Format menu will again appear on the screen.

10. Type "4".

    Right justification has been returned to the default setting, "On". Now your printed document will be aligned against both the left and right margins with the words on each line unevenly spaced.

11. Press <CR>.

    Your document will reappear on the screen.

✔   CHECKPOINT

    c. How do you return to your document from the Print Format menu?

    _____

REVIEW QUESTIONS

1. Which menu is needed to format a printed page?

    _____

2. Your first formatting task should be to visualize how you would like your finished document to look when it is printed. Identify several factors that affect the way your text is arranged on the printed page.

    _____

3.   Explain the meaning of the word "pitch."

4.   WordPerfect offers four different styles for underlining on the Print Format menu. Describe them.

5.   WordPerfect's default setting produces pica type. How can you produce elite type?

6.   Identify the Print Format key.

7.   Proportional spacing can be selected from the same menu option that pitch is. What is proportional spacing?

8.   How will your text be formatted when Right Justification is turned off?

9.   A standard document contains how many lines per vertical inch? How does this change if your document is double-spaced?

DOCUMENTATION RESEARCH

1.   Refer to the user's manual to determine how to adjust the page length if the lines per inch (lpi) is set at eight.

2.   How does double indenting appear on the screen?

SECTION 2

ASSIGNMENTS

1. Create **Track.txt**
2. Review Questions
3. Research Documentation

THE LINE FORMAT MENU

When the Shift-F8 keys are pressed, the Line Format menu appears on your screen (Figure 5-3). This menu offers you several options for changing the format of each line. WordPerfect allows you to change the line format within a document as many times as you like.

Keep in mind that all of the formatting options selected must ultimately fit together to create one document that is both visually appealing and professionally prepared. Therefore, when you choose an option from the Line Format menu, you must always consider how it will affect or be affected by other options from the Format menus.

You may select an option by typing one of the listed numbers.

1 Tabs; 2 E-Tabs; 3 Margins; 4 Spacing; 5 Hyphenation; 6 Align Char: 0

FIGURE 5-3   Line Format Menu.

The Line Format menu options are defined as follows:

   1 Tabs.   The Tabs Setting submenu appears on the screen (Figure 5-4).   Tabs are preset at five-space intervals.

```
Delete EOL (clear tabs); Enter number (set tab); Del (clear tab)
Press EXIT when done.

          10        20        30        40        50        60        70
0123456789012345678901234567890123456789012345678901234567890123456789
T    T    T    T    T    T    T    T    T    T    T    T    T    T    T    T
80        90       100       110       120       130       140       150
0123456789012345678901234567890123456789012345678901234567890123456789
T    T    T    T    T    T    T    T    T    T    T    T    T    T    T    T
```

FIGURE 5-4   Tabs Setting Submenu.

The Tabs Setting submenu:

To clear all previous tab settings, move the cursor to the first tab and press the Ctrl-<End> keys.

To delete one tab, move the cursor to the tab set on the ruler and press <DEL>.

To set new tab stops, move the cursor to the starting point, type "0" (zero), "," (comma), then the interval number.

To set a single tab, move the cursor to the desired position on the Tabs Setting submenu and press <TAB>.

To exit the Tabs Setting submenu, press F7.

2 E-Tabs.   Extended tabs allows you to set tab stops beyond column 158.   A prompt instructs you to type the beginning point for the extended tab (column 158 or beyond) and the interval at which the tabs should be set.

3 Margins.   Left and right margins may be set to any value between 0 and 250. The default settings, 10 and 74, format a 1-inch margin both left and right on 8 1/2-inch-wide paper.   This is the standard setting for pica type (10 pitch).   At this setting sixty-four characters can be printed between margins.

The standard margin settings for elite type (12 pitch) are 12 and 89. At these settings, sixty-seven characters can be printed between 1-inch margins.

When you select this option, the current margin settings are displayed. Enter the values that you want for both the right and the left margins. Remember that the number of characters per horizontal inch is dependent on the pitch you have chosen.

Changing margin settings widens or narrows the line space in which characters are printed. If you change margin settings, it may also be necessary to change tab settings.

4 Spacing. Your document will be single-spaced unless you designate otherwise. You are prompted to type a number to set the spacing between lines. WordPerfect is designed to set spacing in 1/2-line increments. For example, type "2" for double spacing, "3" for triple spacing, ".5" for 1/2-line spacing, or "1.5" for 1 1/2-line spacing.

5 Hyphenation. The Hyphenation menu appears on the screen. Hyphenation is used to improve the appearance of a document by keeping spaces between words more regular; ragged right margins become less ragged, and right-justified margins have less prominent spaces between words.

When you begin hyphenation, WordPerfect guides you through your text, pausing at the end of each line that contains a word that can be hyphenated. WordPerfect indicates a suggested location for placement of a hyphen, then allows you to decide if the division is acceptable.

6 Align Char. An "Align Char=" message appears. This option is used to assign a character on which to vertically line up text. The default is a "." (a decimal point or period). This option is used in combination with the Tab Align key, Ctrl-F6. When Tab Align is used, typed text moves to the left until the alignment character is typed, then text moves to the right as usual. You can change the alignment character any time.

GUIDED ACTIVITY: SETTING MARGINS

In this Guided Activity you set the margins of the fourth and second copies of the **Quote.txt**. Because the second quotation is in 12 pitch, the default settings of 10 and 74 must be changed to 12 and 89 in order to maintain 1-inch margins.

1. Retrieve **Quote.txt** if necessary.

2. Move the cursor to the first word of the fourth copy of the quotation.

3. Press the Shift-F8 keys.

   The Line Format menu will appear on the screen.

4. Type "3".

   The prompt "[Margin Set] 10 74 to Left=" will appear.

5. Type "20".

   The left margin is now set at Pos 20.

6. Press <SPACEBAR>.

7. Type "64".

    The right margin is now set at Pos 64.

8. Press <CR>.

    Your text will reappear on the screen.

9. Move the cursor to the second blank line below the quotation.

    The margins have changed to the new settings.

10. Press the Shift-F8 keys.

    The Line Format menu will appear on the screen.

11. Type "3".

    The Margin Set submenu will appear on the screen.

12. Type "10".

    The left margin is now reset to the default, Pos 10.

13. Press <SPACEBAR>.

14. Type "74".

    The right margin is now reset to the default, Pos 74.

15. Press <CR>.

    The text will reappear on the screen.

16. Type "The above quotation has 2-inch margins (set at 20, 64).".

17. Repeat steps 2 through 15 to change the margins of the second copy of the quotation. Set the left margin at 12 and the right margin at 89.

18. Type "The above quotation has 1-inch margins (set at 12, 89)." on the line below "The above quotation is in 12 pitch.".

19. Save and Print Quote.txt.

    The printed document will look like that in Figure 5-5.

✔ CHECKPOINT

a.   Which keystrokes are used to access the Line Format menu?

_____

b.   When you change margin settings, how is that change displayed on the screen?

_____

What You Have Accomplished

You have changed the margin settings of the fourth quotation on your document so that it will be printed with 2-inch-wide margins. You have also changed the margin settings in the second copy of the quotation to maintain 1-inch-wide margins when the pitch is set to 12.   Margins can be reset any time during the course of typing a document.

MARGIN RELEASE

To type text within the left margin, press the Shift-<TAB> keys. Each time you press these keys, the cursor jumps one tab stop to the left, even into the left margin.

GUIDED ACTIVITY: CHANGING TAB SETTINGS

1.   Display a clear screen.

2.   Press the Shift-F8 keys.

     The Line Format menu will appear.

3.   Type "1".

     The Tabs Setting submenu will appear

4.   Press the Ctrl-<End> keys.

     All of the tabs from the cursor forward have been deleted.

5.   Type "15".

6.   Press <CR>.

     Your first tab stop is set at Pos 15.

7.   Type "35".

```
If you treat a man as he is, you make him worse than he is.  If
you treat him as if he already were what he potentially could be,
you make him what he should be.         Goethe

The above quotation is in 10 pitch.



If you treat a man as he is, you make him worse than he is.  If you treat him
as if he already were what he potentially could be, you make him what he
should be.         Goethe

The above quotation is in 12 pitch.
The above quotation has 1-inch margins (set at 12, 89).



If you treat a man as he is, you make him worse than he is.  If
you treat him as if he already were what he potentially could be,
you make him what he should be.         Goethe

The above quotation is left-justified only.



          If you treat a man as he is, you make him
          worse than he is.  If you treat him as if he
          already were what he potentially could be,
          you make him what he should be.       Goethe

The above quotation has 2-inch margins (set at 20, 64).
```

FIGURE 5-5 **Quote.txt** (Revised).

8. Press <CR>.

    A tab stop will be set at Pos 35.

9. Type "55".

10. Press <CR>.

    A tab stop will be set at Pos 55.

11. Type "65".

12.   Press <CR>.

A tab stop will be set at Pos 65.

13.   Press F7 to Exit the Tabs Setting submenu.

✔   CHECKPOINT

c.   What keystrokes are required to access the Tabs Setting submenu?

_____

d.   Describe the steps required to remove all existing tabs.

_____

e.   Identify the keystroke that allows you to exit the Tabs Setting submenu and return to the text.

_____

Hint: The process of using submenus can at first be confusing, especially when a program is designed with multiple layers of submenus.   Just remember that each menu choice follows a predesigned path, and that your computer will do nothing that you do not command it to do.   In addition, WordPerfect is designed to lead you through each submenu by providing prompts on the submenu screens.   There is always a way back from a submenu to the main menu.

GUIDED ACTIVITY: USING TAB SETTINGS

1.   Type the text in Figure 5-6 using the <TAB> key to move the cursor horizontally across the line to each Tab stop.   Press <CR> at the end of each line.

2.   Save the document with the name "Track.txt".

GUIDED ACTIVITY: CHANGING LINE SPACING

1.   Retrieve Track.txt if necessary.

2.   Move the cursor to the first line of track records.

3.   Press the Shift-F8 keys.

The Line Format menu will appear.

4.   Type "4".

A prompt will direct you to type a number to change the line space setting.

```
BOY'S RECORD TRACK TIMES, 5K RUN

 1 TOM HOLMES          SIBLEY             14.33    1972
 2 BRETT PALMER        NORTH ST. PAUL     14.41    1972
 3 MIKE JOHNSON        MARINER            14.48    1978
 4 DON JEFFERS         WHITE BEAR         14.53    1971
 5 SKIP NELSEN         RAMSEY             14.54    1972
 6 ANTON PETERSON      NORTH ST. PAUL     14.55    1979
 7 LARRY BLACK         STILLWATER         14.57    1976
 8 JIM HAYDEN          SIBLEY             14.57    1974
 9 DAVID ROBERTS       BLAINE             14.58    1976
10 JERRY MARTIN        ANOKA              14.59    1976
11 BILL PLUMB          MARINER            14.59    1978
12 DICK ANDERSON       MARINER            14.59    1978
```

FIGURE 5-6   Track.txt.

5. Typé "1.5".

    You have chosen to set line spacing to 1 1/2 lines.

6. Press <CR>.

    Your text will appear double-spaced on the screen. The "Ln" number in the
    status line will display the line on which the cursor is actually resting.

7. Save and Print **Track.txt**.

    When you printed the **Track.txt** file, it contained 1 1/2 line spaces between
    each line.

✔ CHECKPOINT

    f.   What keystrokes are needed to format text for 1 1/2 line spacing?

    g.   How does the screen display change to reflect a line-space setting of
         1 1/2 lines?

What You Have Accomplished

You used the Tab Settings submenu to change tab settings; then typed several columns of information with the new tab settings.   You also changed the line spacing in your document to 1 1/2 lines.

REVIEW QUESTIONS

1.   Which keys access the Line Format menu?

   _____

2.   Describe how to change the tab settings within a document.

   _____

3.   How would you go about setting wider margins in your document?

   _____

4.   Describe the procedure for setting line spacing to double spacing.   How does this change appear on the screen?

   _____

5.   What is a menu?   a submenu?

   _____

DOCUMENTATION RESEARCH

1.   Suppose that your document contains a list of numbers with decimal places. What is the most efficient way to format your document so that the decimal points are vertically aligned?

   _____

2.   Describe how WordPerfect's Hyphenation feature works.

   _____

3.   What is a "soft hyphen"?

   _____

4.   Under what circumstances would you use the E-Tabs feature?   What is the default setting for E-Tabs?

   _____

SECTION 3

ASSIGNMENTS

1. Edit Educate.txt
2. Review Questions
3. Research Documentation

THE PAGE FORMAT MENU

When the Alt-F8 keys are pressed, the Page Format menu (Figure 5-7) appears on your screen. The options on this menu affect the size of the printed page. With this menu you can set top and bottom margins, assign a page number position, and include headers and footers. This menu can be used to format the pages in an entire document or to format pages individually. None of the options from the Page Format menu appear on the screen, but they will be included in your final printed document.

You may select a Page Format option by typing one of the listed numbers.

```
Page Format

    1 - Page Number Position

    2 - New Page Number

    3 - Center Page Top to Bottom

    4 - Page Length

    5 - Top Margin

    6 - Headers or Footers

    7 - Page Number Column Positions

    8 - Suppress for Current page only

    9 - Conditional End of Page

    A - Widow/Orphan

Selection: 0
```

FIGURE 5-7 Page Format Menu.

The Page Format menu options are defined as follows:

1 Page Number Position.   You can select one of nine page number positions. The Position of Page Number on Page submenu (Figure 5-8) appears.   If you keep the default setting, no page numbers are printed.

```
Position of Page Number on Page

   0 - No page numbers

   1 - Top left of every page

   2- Top center of every page

   3 - Top right of every page

   4 - Top alternating left & right

   5 - Bottom left of every page

   6 - Bottom center of every page

   7 - Bottom right of every page

   8 - Bottom alternating left & right

Selection: 0
```

FIGURE 5-8   Position of Page Number on Page Submenu.

2 New Page Number.   The prompt "New Page #:" appears at the bottom of the screen.   This option renumbers pages by inserting a new page numbering code.   It allows you to choose between arabic and roman styles.

3 Center Page Top to Bottom.   This option allows you to center text vertically, that is, to format a page so that a printed document has equal top and bottom margins.   This is useful for very short letters that take up only a small amount of space on standard size paper.

4 Page Length.   A Page Length submenu (Figure 5-9) appears.   This submenu allows you to change the page length by changing the number of text lines on a page.   The default setting is sixty-six lines per page, which is six lines per inch on standard 11-inch paper.   The default margin setting places a 1-inch margin (12 lines altogether) at the top and bottom of the page; therefore only fifty-four lines are available for text.

```
Page Length

    1 - Letter Size Paper:  Form Length = 66 lines (11 inches)
          Single Spaced Text Lines = 54 (This includes lines
          used for Headers, Footers and/or page numbers.)

    2 - Legal Size Paper:  Form Length = 84 lines (14 inches)
          Single Spaced Text Lines = 72 (This includes lines
          used for Headers, Footers and/or page numbers.)

    3 - Other (Maximum page length = 108 lines)

Current Settings

    Form Length in lines (6 per inch):  66

    Number of Single Spaced Text Lines:  54


Selection: 0
```

FIGURE 5-9   Page Length Submenu.

5 Top Margin. This option allows you to reset the top margin in 1/2-line
    increments for more intricate formatting with different type and sizes
    of fonts. The default setting instructs the printer to skip 1 inch
    (twelve 1/2-lines) before printing.

6 Headers or Footers. The Header/Footer Specification submenu (Figure 5-10)
    appears. A header is information placed at the top of the page. A
    footer is information placed at the bottom. Neither headers nor
    footers are part of the regular text. WordPerfect allows you to format
    two headers and two footers per page, but they must be placed in
    different locations (e.g., one header at the left margin and one at the
    right). You may also alternate the position of the headers and footers
    on odd- and even-numbered pages.

```
Header/Footer Specification

   Type                           Occurrence
   1 - Header A                   0 - Discontinue
   2 - Header B                   1 - Every Page
   3 - Footer A                   2 - Odd Pages
   4 - Footer B                   3 - Even Pages
                                  4 - Edit

   Selection:  0                  Selection:  0
```

FIGURE 5-10   Header/Footer Specification Submenu.

7 Page Number Column Positions.   The Page Number Column Positions submenu
   (Figure 5-11) appears. With this submenu, you can designate the exact
   position of a page number. The default settings are L=10, C=42, and
   R=74.

```
Reset Column Position for Page Numbers

   (L = Left Corner, C = Center, R = Right Corner)

         1 - Set to Initial Settings (In tenths of an inch)
                L=10 C=42 R=74

         2 - Set to Specified Settings

Current Settings

   L=10 C=42 R=74

Selection:  0
```

FIGURE 5-11   Page Number Column Positions Submenu.

8 Suppress for Current Page Only. The Suppress for Current Page Only submenu
   (Figure 5-12) appears. With this submenu you can turn off any
   combination of page formats on the current page only. This feature is
   useful for temporarily removing headers or footers.

```
Suppress Page Format for Current Page Only

    To temporarily turn off multiple items, include a "+" between menu entries.
    For example 5+6+2 will turn off Header A, Header B, and Page Numbering
    for the current page.

    1 - Turn off all page numbering, headers and footers

    2 - Turn page numbering off

    3 - Print page number at bottom center (this page only)

    4 - Turn off all headers and footers

    5 - Turn off Header A

    6 - Turn off Header B

    7 - Turn off Footer A

    8 - Turn off Footer B

Selection(s):
```

FIGURE 5-12   Suppress Page Format for Current Page Only Submenu.

9 Conditional End of Page. The prompt "Number of lines to keep together ="
   appears. This option allows you to keep a designated block of text
   together on the same page. In other words, if a page end occurs in the
   middle of a body of text that should appear on one page, such as a
   quotation, you can command the computer to move the entire quotation to
   the next page. This feature is useful for avoiding problems during
   major revisions.

A Widow/Orphan. The prompt "Widow/Orphan Protect (Y/N): N" appears on the
   bottom of the screen. This option allows you to prevent a single line
   of a paragraph from being stranded on a page. WordPerfect defines a
   widow line as the first line of a paragraph left alone at the bottom of
   one page while the rest of the paragraph is on the following page. An
   orphan line is defined as the last line of a paragraph left alone at
   the top of one page while the rest of the paragraph is located on the
   preceding page. The default setting is "N".

GUIDED ACTIVITY: CREATING HEADERS

1. Retrieve the file Educate.txt from the WordPerfect Student Data disk.

2. Move the cursor to the top of the first page of Educate.txt.

3. Press the Alt-F8 keys.

    The Page Format menu will appear on your screen.

4. Type "6".

    The Header/Footer Specification submenu will appear on your screen.

5. Type "1".

    Header A has been chosen.

6. Type "2".

    You have chosen to place your header on odd-numbered pages. A blank screen
    will appear.

7. Type "Printer Formatting".

    This is the header that will be printed on odd-numbered pages.

8. Press the F7 key.

    The Page Format menu will reappear on your screen. Your header has been
    saved.

9. Type "6".

    The Header/Footer Specification submenu will reappear on your screen.

10. Type "2".

    You have chosen a second header.

11. Type "3".

    You have chosen to place Header B on even-numbered pages. A blank screen
    will appear.

12. Type "WordPerfect".

    This is the header that will appear on even-numbered pages.

13. Press the F7 key.

     The Page Format menu will reappear. Header B has been saved.

14. Press <CR>.

     Your text will reappear on the screen. The headers you chose will not be visible on the screen, but they will be included on the printed document.

What You Have Accomplished

You have used the Page Format menu to include two different headers on your document. One of the headers will be printed on even-numbered pages and one will be printed on odd-numbered pages. You have also learned that the F7 key saves the headers you have chosen.

✔ CHECKPOINT

   a. Identify the keystrokes that access the Page Format Menu.

   _____

   b. Describe how the Headers/Footers Specification submenu is used to place headers on even-numbered pages.

   _____

Hint: When you are creating headers or footers, you may also make use of other WordPerfect features such as boldfacing, underlining, centering, or placing text flush right. Press the appropriate keys before you enter the header or footer information on the Headers/Footers Specification submenu.

GUIDED ACTIVITY: CHANGING THE PAGE NUMBER

1. Press the Alt-F8 keys.

    The Page Format menu will appear on your screen.

2. Type "2".

    The prompt "New Page #:" will appear on your screen.

3. Type "26". Press <CR>.

    The prompt "Numbering Style 1 Arabic; 2 Roman: 0" will appear on your screen.

4.   Type "2" to choose Roman numerals.

5.   Press <CR>.

Your document will reappear on the screen. The new page number will appear in the status line. If you Reveal Codes by pressing the Alt-F3 keys, you will see the embedded code for the new page number in Roman numerals.

GUIDED ACTIVITY: INSERTING A PAGE NUMBER AT THE BOTTOM CENTER OF EACH PAGE

1.   Press the Alt-F8 keys.

The Page Format menu will appear on your screen.

2.   Type "1".

The Position of Page Number on Page submenu will appear on your screen.

3.   Type "6".

You have chosen to place a page number at the bottom center of every page of the document.

4.   Press <CR>.

Your document will reappear on the screen. The page numbers will not be visible on the screen, but they will be included in the printed document.

✔ CHECKPOINT

c. Which keystrokes are required to select a format for numbering pages?

GUIDED ACTIVITY: USING THE WIDOW/ORPHAN FEATURE

1.   Press the Alt-F8 keys to access the Page Format menu.

2.   Type "A".

This prompt will appear at the bottom of your screen:
"Widow/Orphan Protect (Y/N): N"

3.   Type "Y".

Your document will not be printed with widow or orphan lines.

4. Press <CR>.

Your text will reappear on the screen.

5. Press Shift-F7.

The Print menu will appear on your screen.

6. Type "1".

The full text of your document will be printed.

7. Press F7 to Save and Exit.

8. Examine the printed document to determine if the printer did indeed include the page-formatting instructions. If it did not, first check to see if your printer supports the page-formatting features you used. Then try reworking the Guided Activities to determine if you issued all commands correctly.

✔ CHECKPOINT

d. What keystrokes are required to command the computer to format a document without widow or orphan lines?

GUIDED ACTIVITY: CENTERING A PAGE VERTICALLY

1. Retrieve Olson.ltr.

2. Move the cursor to the top of Olson.ltr.

3. Press the Alt-F8 keys to access the Page Format menu.

4. Type "3".

You have chosen to center Olson.ltr on your printed page.

5. Press <CR>.

Olson.ltr will reappear. It will not appear centered on the screen, but it will be centered vertically when it is printed.

6. Press Shift-F7.

The Print menu will appear on your screen.

7.   Type "1".

The full text of your document will be printed.

✔ CHECKPOINT

e.   What keystrokes did you need to center the page vertically?

_____

What You Have Accomplished

In following this unit's Guided Activites, you have created two headers, inserted page numbers at the bottom center of each page, and then instructed the computer to eliminate widow and orphan lines from your document, **Educate.txt.**   You have also centered **Olson.ltr** vertically on a page.   You also printed **Educate.txt** and **Olson.ltr** to see the results of your page-formatting commands and you experimented with your printer to find out which WordPerfect features it can accommodate.

REVIEW QUESTIONS

1.   Identify the keystrokes required to access the Page Format menu.

_____

2.   There are ten options on the Page Format menu.   Identify the option you would choose to keep together the text lines of a quotation that you do not want printed on separate pages.

_____

3.   What are headers?   Where are they located on a printed document?

_____

4.   Suppose that you are creating a document that must be printed on legal size rather than standard size paper.   How would you go about formatting a page to include additional lines of text?

_____

5.   What commands must you give the computer to avoid printing the first or last line of a paragraph alone on a page?

_____

6. Suppose that you are creating a document with headers but do not want to include the headers on your title page. How would you go about suppressing those headers for that page alone?

———————————————————

7. WordPerfect provides a number of options for positioning page numbers on a page. What procedure is required to position numbers at the bottom center of every page?

———————————————————

8. How do you use the Suppress for Current Page Only submenu to turn off more than one Page Format item?

———————————————————

9. Suppose that you are typing a rather short letter and would like the text of the letter centered on a page. How do you use the Page Format menu to accomplish this task?

———————————————————

10. The changes you make with the Page Format menu are not revealed until your document is printed. If the changes you specify do not appear in the printed document, what steps should you take to determine why not?

———————————————————

11. Formatting options are limited by the capabilities of your printer. How can you learn more about the printer?

———————————————————

DOCUMENTATION RESEARCH

1. Under what circumstances would you choose the Conditional End of Page feature instead of the Widow/Orphan feature to keep text lines together?

———————————————————

2. How does resetting the top margin affect headers and footers? text lines?

———————————————————

3. How do you insert a page number in headers and footers?

———————————————————

APPLICATION

B

1. WordPerfect program disk
2. WordPerfect Learning disk
3. WordPerfect Student Data disk
4. printer

ASSIGNMENTS

The assignments to be completed for this Application section are

1. Create **Artmemo.txt**
2. Create **Piano.txt**
3. Create **Legal.ltr**
4. Create **Schedule.txt**
5. Create **Reminder.txt**

APPLICATIONS

This Application section contains a number of documents that can be reproduced to apply the skills you have acquired in Units 1 through 5. Format your documents so that they look like the ones on the printed pages of this section. Some format instructions have been handwritten on the pages of this section to guide you. Remember that right justification does not appear on the screen, it appears when a document is printed

Use your template and the Quick Reference card to find the keystroke commands and menus you need. Remember that there is often more than one keystroke choice that can be used to create and format a document. Your primary task is to find the most efficient way to reproduce the documents.

You may also want to create your own applications—some tasks that are more meaningful to your everyday work. Your WordPerfect Student Data disk should have plenty of space available to store additional documents.

Boldface topic headings.

DATE: (today's date)

FROM: Steve Johnson
                Room 365
                Lakewood School

TO: All Teaching Staff

SUBJECT: "Beyond the Horizon" publication

I know that all of you have many student writings and drawings that you would like to see in the "Beyond the Horizon" publication. We are interested in putting together a representative selection of students' work. Please see that you get as many of the articles and drawings to my office as you can before the first of May. We are excited at the prospect of our first student publication.

12 pitch

Reset left margins to 24

Reset right margin to 81

Name this document Artmemo.txt

Use the <ESC> key to produce these asterisks.

****

Center each line horizontally

<u>BEGINNING IN SEPTEMBER</u>

<u>PRIVATE PIANO LESSONS</u>

<u>Beginner and Intermediate Levels</u>

<u>Harold Hill, Teacher</u>

<u>2602 Sherwood Way</u>

Graduate of Hill Academy of Music, Gary, Indiana

Experienced in private piano instruction

*Taught elementary and secondary music in private

and public schools*

(flush right)   For more information, call 636-7281

****

Center this document vertically on the page.

Name this document Piano.txt

ZACH, PETERSON, NELSON & JONES
Attorneys at Law
Law Building
445 East Main Street
Lancaster, Ohio 46783

Thomas A. Zach
Mildred F. Peterson
Henry A. Nelson
Sandra E. Jones

Lancaster 312/758-3652
Metro Line 312/445-3697

flush right

August 26, 1986

To: Ms. Lynn Jacobsen
       Mr. John Taylor
       Mr. Peter Taylor
       Mr. Scott Taylor
       Mr. Kenneth Taylor
       Mr. Jason Evert

12 pitch
left margin 12
right margin 93

Re: Estate of Paul T. Taylor

Dear Mr. Taylor:

This is to inform you that I have been retained to probate the estate of Paul T. Taylor.

I have enclosed to each of you copies of the following documents:

1.   Last Will and Testament of Paul T. Taylor, dated August 19, 1975.
2.   Petition for Formal Probate of Will and for Formal Appointment of Executor.
3.   Order and Notice of Hearing.

As you will note by reviewing the Will, Paul Taylor had nominated Henry R. Gold, Sr., as the Personal Representative of this Estate. Mr. Gold, who now lives in Colorado, and will be signing a Renunciation to act in that capacity.

Ms. Lynn Jacobsen, the only living child of Paul Taylor, has petitioned to have herself appointed as the Personal Representative of the Estate. This petition will be heard by the Court in accordance with the enclosed Order on Monday, September 16, 1986, at 1:30 P.M. in County Court in Stoneville.

All heirs are invited to attend this hearing. The only one legally required to attend, however, is Ms. Lynn Jacobsen.

If you have any questions regarding the progress of this estate, Mr. Taylor, please feel free to contact me.

Thank you.

Yours Truly,
Zach, Peterson, Nelson & Jones

Sandra E. Jones

Enclosures

Search for Mr. Taylor; replace with Mr. Evert

Name this document Legal.doc

Name this document Schedule.txt

Center heading

SOUTH SUBURBAN FITNESS CENTER
2168 CENTURY DRIVE
LINCOLN, NEBRASKA 68341
693-2014

12 pitch
left margin 12
right margin 93

The South Suburban Fitness Center is offering a series of fitness classes beginning this fall. The purpose of each class is to give you a sense of overall well-being by increasing your strength, endurance, and flexibility. Each class is designed to fill your individual needs and match your fitness level. The Fitness staff recommends that you spend six to twelve weeks in each level before advancing.

Center Heading

FITNESS CLASS SCHEDULE

Tabs at 20, 50, 70

CLASS	LEVEL	TIMES
Total Body Workout	Beginner	8-9 a.m., MWF 7-8 p.m., TTh
Total Body Workout 1	Intermediate	10-11 a.m., TTh 8-9 a.m., Sat
Aerobics 1	Beginner/ Intermediate	10-11 a.m., MWF 7-8 p.m., MW
Flex and Tone	Advanced	10-11 a.m., TTh 8-9 a.m., Sat
Fitness over Fifty	Beginner	8-9 a.m., MWF 7-8 p.m., TTh

Call 693-2014 to register.

Be sure to wear comfortable clothing and appropriate shoes for each class.

TO: _____

R E M I N D E R

This note is to remind you that you are scheduled
to work at the Fall Supper on November 4 from
_____ .

All   food   should   be   delivered   by   noon   on
November 4.   Thank you for volunteering to bring
_____ .

Thank you.

Fall Supper Committee

Margins
Left 24
Right 72

Instructions
   Copy this reminder three more times.
Insert a hard page break between each
reminder. Fill in the blank lines as
you like.

Name this document Reminder.txt

UNIT

6

CONTROLLING THE PRINTER

SUPPLIES NEEDED

1. WordPerfect program disk
2. WordPerfect Student Data disk
3. printer

OBJECTIVES

After completing this unit, you will be able to

1. print multiple copies;
2. print a block of text;
3. print a page of text;
4. use the Printer Control menu to stop, resume, and cancel print jobs.

IMPORTANT KEYSTROKES

Shift-F7...........................to use the Print menu

ASSIGNMENTS

1. Print Wordperf.txt
2. Print Forfun
3. Print Olson.ltr
4. Review Questions
5. Research Documentation

PRINTING

In Unit 5 you made some decisions about how you wanted the text of your document arranged on the printed page. You learned that some formatting decisions are related to the type of printer you are using. In Unit 6 you discover how to control the printer so that it prints your documents the way you want.

Units 5 and 6 should be used in close association with one another. Learning more about your printer will help you to use the formatting options that WordPerfect provides. Learning more about formatting options will help you to make full use of your printer's capabilities.

Printing can be the most frustrating part of learning to use a word-processing program. Keep in mind, though, that the troubles you encounter usually have simple solutions. The most common printing problems are the result of incorrect commands sent from the computer to the printer. Therefore it is important that you think through each command that you embed in the document you are editing.

Sometimes printing problems are the result of a damaged disk; this is why you should always have backup copies of both program disks and data storage disks.

Occasionally a printing problem is caused by the printer itself. Check the obvious. Is the printer plugged in and set up properly? Is it supplied with paper?

THE PRINT MENU

When you press the Shift-F7 keys, the Print menu (Figure 6-1) appears on your screen. The Print menu allows you to control the actions of your printer. You can print one or more than one copy, number pages as you like, or select the printer you want to perform your printing tasks. You can also queue print jobs to print in an assigned order while you edit another document.

You may select a print option by typing one of the listed numbers.

```
1 Full Text; 2 Page; 3 Change Options; 4 Printer Control; 5 Type-thru: 0
```

FIGURE 6-1   Print Menu.

The Print menu options are defined as follows:

1 Full Text. A "Please wait" prompt appears in place of the Print menu and the entire document, that is, all pages, are printed.

2 Page. A "Please wait" prompt appears in place of the Print menu and the current page of text (the one shown in the status line) is printed.

3 Change Print Options. The Change Print Options Temporarily submenu (Figure 6-2) appears on the screen. The options on this menu affect the current print job only.

```
Change Print Options Temporarily

1 - Printer Number              1

2 - Number of Copies            1

3 - Binding Width (1/10 in.)    0

Selection:  0
```

FIGURE 6-2   Change Print Options Temporarily Submenu.

The options on this submenu are defined as follows:

1 Printer Number. If you have more than one printer attached to your computer, this option allows you to designate a printer. The default is 1.

2 Number of Copies. This option allows you to choose the number of copies printed. It is preset to one, so unless you designate otherwise, each time you issue a print command your printer will print one copy of your document.

3 Binding Width (1/10 in.). This option allows you to determine whether or not the page numbers are to be shifted right on odd-numbered pages and left on even-numbered pages. It is a useful feature for those documents that you want to bind.

4 Printer Control. The Printer Control submenu (Figure 6-3) appears on the screen. You can select an option by typing one of the listed numbers or letters.

```
Printer Control

   1 - Select Print Options        C - Cancel Print Job(s)
   2 - Display Printers and Fonts  D - Display All Print Jobs
   3 - Select Printers             G - "Go" (Resume Printing)
                                   P - Print a Document
Selection: 0                       R - Rush Print Job
                                   S - Stop Printing


Current Job

Job Number: n/a                    Page Number: n/a
Job Status: n/a                    Current Copy: n/a
Message:      The print queue is empty

Job List

Job Document          Destination          Forms and Print Options

Additional jobs not shown:  0
```

FIGURE 6-3   Printer Control Submenu.

The Printer Control submenu options are defined as follows:

1 Select Print Options. The printer number, number of copies, or binding width can be changed with this option. This is different from option 3 on the Print menu in that the selections you make from this submenu affect all print jobs until you exit WordPerfect.

2 Display Printers and Fonts. A list of six printer definitions appears along with eight available fonts (type styles) for each printer.

3 Select Printers. This submenu option allows you to add printers to your list and to specify the type of paper used (e.g., continuous feed, single-sheet forms)

C Cancel Print Job(s). One or all print jobs can be cancelled.

D Display All Print Jobs. The Job List, that is, all jobs waiting to be sent to the printer, is displayed.

G "Go" (Resume Printing). If the printer has been stopped (option S), this command will direct it to start printing again. Printing restarts at the beginning of a document.

P Print a Document. A document that has been saved on a disk can be printed without first being retrieved. The pages that you want printed can be specified.

R Rush Print Job. The priority of a document waiting on the Job List can be changed so that it is printed immediately.

S Stop Printing. The printer stops printing but print jobs are not cancelled. This command is useful when the paper runs out or jams, or when a ribbon needs replacing. Select option G to restart.

5 Type-thru. The printer may be used like a typewriter. It can print either a character or a line at a time as it is being typed at the microcomputer keyboard.

GUIDED ACTIVITY: PRINTING TWO COPIES OF A SINGLE PAGE

1. Retrieve **Wordperf.txt**.

2. Press the Shift-F7 keys.

    The Print menu will appear on your screen.

3. Type "3".

    The Change Print Options Temporarily submenu will appear on the screen. The cursor is flashing next to the word "Selection."

4. Type "2".

    The cursor has moved beside the Number of Copies option on this submenu.

5. Type "2".

    The printer will be commanded to print two copies of your document.

6. Press <CR> twice.

    The cursor will return to its original location next to the word "Selection."
    Then the Print menu will reappear on your screen.

7. Make sure your printer is turned on and set up properly.

8. Type "2".

A "Please wait" prompt will appear at the bottom of your screen and in a few seconds the printer will begin to print the page on which your cursor was resting. When one copy is finished the printer will automatically feed the paper up to the top of the next page and print another copy.

What You Have Accomplished

You have learned that the Shift-F7 keys allow you to access the Print menu, from which you can control the actions of your printer. You have also learned that the Change Print Options Temporarily submenu lets you designate the number of copies to be printed. You directed your printer to print two copies of a single page.

✔ CHECKPOINT

a. Which keystrokes are needed to access the Print menu?

_____

b. Describe how to command your printer to print two copies of a document.

_____

c. What is the procedure for printing a single page of a document?

_____

GUIDED ACTIVITY: PRINTING A BLOCK OF TEXT

1. Move the cursor to the beginning of the second paragraph in Wordperf.txt.

2. Press the Alt-F4 keys.

The Block function has been turned on.

3. Move the cursor to the bottom line of the second paragraph.

The second paragraph is now highlighted.

4. Press the Shift-F7 keys.

The Print menu will appear on the screen. The prompt "Print Block (Y/N) N" will appear at the bottom of your screen.

5. Type "Y".

    The highlighted text will be printed.

6. Press the Alt-F4 keys to toggle off Block.

✔ CHECKPOINT

    d. Which keys are used to highlight a block of text for printing?

    _____

    e. What is the default value for the Number of Copies option on the Change
        Print Options Temporarily submenu?

    _____

GUIDED ACTIVITY: STOPPING AND RESTARTING A PRINT JOB

1. Retrieve Olson.ltr.

2. Press the Shift-F7 keys.

    The Print menu will appear on your screen.

3. Type "2".

    The page on which the cursor was resting will be printed. After a few lines
    have been printed, stop the print job.

4. Press the Shift-F7 keys to display the Print menu.

5. Type "4" to display the Printer Control submenu.

6. Type "S".

    The printer will stop printing.

7. Advance the printer paper to the top of the next page before continuing.

8. Type "G".

    The printer will resume printing from the beginning of the page.

9. Press <CR>.

    Your document will reappear on the screen.

✔ CHECKPOINT

    f.   What keystrokes are needed to command the printer to stop printing a document?

---

    g.   How can you restart the printer after you have stopped it?

GUIDED ACTIVITY: PRINTING A DOCUMENT STORED ON A DATA DISK

1.   Press the Shift-F7 keys to display the Print menu.

2.   Type "4" to display the Printer Control submenu.

3.   Type "P".

The prompt "Document name" will appear on the screen.

4.   Type "Forfun".

5.   Press <CR>.

The prompt "Starting page: 1" will appear on your screen.

6.   Press <CR>.

You have accepted the default page (1), which will be the first page printed. (When you want to begin printing on another page, type that page number after the prompt.)

The prompt, "Ending page:", will appear on the screen.

7.   Press <CR>.

You have accepted the default page (1), which will be the last page printed. **Forfun** has been placed in the Job List that is on the Printer control menu. Since it is only one page long, the entire document will be printed.

✔ CHECKPOINT

    h.   What keystrokes are required to print a document directly from its storage location on a data disk?

---

i.   How does the Printer Control submenu allow you to print a partial document?

GUIDED ACTIVITY: CANCELLING A PRINT JOB

1.   Type "P" to select the Print a Document option from the Printer Control submenu.

     The prompt "Document name:" will appear.

2.   Type "Olson.ltr".

3.   Press <CR>.

     The prompt "Starting page: 1" will appear.

4.   Press <CR>.

     The printer has been directed to start printing on Pg 1. The prompt "Ending page:" will appear.

5.   Press <CR>.

     Olson.ltr has been placed in the Job List and will be printed.

     After a few lines have printed, cancel the print job.

6.   Type "C".

     The prompt "Cancel which job?" (* = All Jobs)" will appear on the Printer Control submenu screen.

7.   Type "1".

     "1" is the job number listed next to Olson.ltr.

8.   Press <CR>.

     The print job, Olson.ltr, has been erased from the job list. Print instructions have also been cancelled and must be reentered in order to print the document. Therefore, typing "G" after commanding the printer to Cancel will not restart your printer.

What You Have Accomplished

You have used the Print menu to print a file directly from your data disk. You have learned that you can direct your printer to start and stop printing on any page. You have also learned how to stop, restart, and cancel a print job.

✔ CHECKPOINT

j. How do you cancel a print job?

Hint: Stop printing when you need to fix a problem with the printer itself (e.g., to change the ribbon or realign the paper).

Cancel printing when a document is not being printed in the format you expect It will probably be necessary to start over with new printing instructions. When you cancel a print job, it is best to turn off the power on your printer and then turn it on again. The printer's memory needs to be cleared so that signals will not be distorted when new commands are given. Remember to set the printer to top-of-form before turning it back on again.

REVIEW QUESTIONS

1. What happens to a print job after you have issued the Cancel command?

2. How does the printer respond when you choose the Page option (2) on the Print menu?

3. Suppose that you need six copies of a document for a meeting. How do you use the Print menu to obtain these copies?

4. It is possible to control the printer to print only one paragraph on a page. Explain how this can be done.

5. Which keystrokes are needed to access the Print menu?

6. How can you terminate a print job after printing has begun?

_____

7. The Printer Control submenu contains a Job List. Explain what a Job List is.

_____

8. It is possible to retrieve and print a document that has been stored on a data disk. Which submenu is needed to accomplish this task?

_____

9. What is the meaning of the term "Type-thru" as listed on the Print menu?

_____

10. Explain the difference between the Stop command and the Cancel command on the Printer Control submenu.

_____

DOCUMENTATION RESEARCH

1. Describe the procedure for printing only a few pages of a long document directly from your data disk.

_____

2. What does the printer do with the document it is currently printing when a Rush Print Job command is given?

_____

3. Which option should you select from the Print menu to change print options for the current print job?

_____

4. Information about the status of the current print job is displayed on the Printer Control submenu. Examine this menu to find out what information is contained under the Current Job heading.

_____

UNIT

7 DISCOVERING MORE WORDPERFECT FUNCTIONS

SUPPLIES NEEDED

1. WordPerfect program disk
2. WordPerfect Student Data disk
3. printer

OBJECTIVES

After completing this unit, you will be able to

1. insert the current date anywhere in a document;
2. indent a paragraph from either margin;
3. use the <ESC> (Escape) key to repeat a character;
4. use the Super/Subscript menu to print text above or below regular text;
5. use the Search feature to find specific words;
6. use the Replace feature to find and replace specific words;
7. use the Footnote/Endnote feature to format footnotes;
8. use the Tab Ruler.

IMPORTANT KEYSTROKES

1. Shift-F5...........to insert the current date
2. F4................to indent text from the left margin
3. Shift-F4..........to indent text from both the left and right margins
4. <ESC> key.........to repeat a character or feature a specified number of times
5. Shift-F1..........to print text 1/2 line above or below regular text
6. Shift-F1..........to superscript or subscript characters
7. F2................to search for text
8. Alt-F2............to replace text with other text
9. Ctrl-F7...........to format footnotes or endnotes
10. Ctrl-F3...........to display the Tab Ruler

ASSIGNMENTS

1. Create Clarke.txt
2. Edit Wordperf.txt
3. Edit Educate.txt
4. Review Questions
5. Research Documentation

DEFAULT VALUES

A **default** is the initial value (or startup setting) that a program assumes each time it is started. Default values are preset by software manufacturers, who make certain assumptions about the standards required by program users.   Default settings are changed by embedding a code in an individual document at the exact location of the desired changes. The changed setting affects only the document currently being edited.

THE DATE AND TIME FEATURE

WordPerfect provides a Date and Time feature that automatically inserts the current date and/or time. When you activate the Date and Time feature, a Date menu appears on your screen. From this menu, you can choose the location and format of the date and time. Option 3 allows you to embed a function code that automatically updates your document each time it is retrieved or printed.

If you fail to enter the date and time when you load the program, January 1, 1980, and the time transpired since boot-up, is inserted into the text.

The Date Menu

When you press Shift-F5, the Date menu (Figure 7-1) appears. You can select an option by typing one of the listed numbers.

```
Date 1 Insert text; 2 Format; 3 Insert Function: 0
```

FIGURE 7-1   Date Menu.

The options on this menu are defined as follows:

   1 Insert text. The date you entered when you loaded WordPerfect is inserted
      wherever the cursor is positioned.

   2 Format. A Format submenu (Figure 7-2) appears. This submenu displays the
      various formats from which you can choose a pattern to display the date
      and/or time. When you do not make a choice, the program chooses the
      default pattern, which is the name of the month, the date, and the
      year; for example, "December 31, 1986".

```
Date Format

    Number    Meaning
       1         Day of the month
       2         Month (number)
       3         Month (word)
       4         Year (all four digits)
       5         Year (last two digits)
       6         Day of the week (word)
       7         Hour (24 Hour Clock)
       8         Hour (12 Hour Clock)
       9         Minute
       0         am / pm

Examples:   3 1, 4       =December 25, 1984
            2/1/5  (6)  =12/25/84 (Tuesday)
            8:90         =10:55am

Date Format  3 1, 4
```

FIGURE 7-2   Format Submenu.

   3 Insert Function. A code is inserted to automatically display the current
      date each time you retrieve or print a document.

GUIDED ACTIVITY: INSERTING THE DATE AUTOMATICALLY

1. Display a clear screen.

2. Press <CR> five times.

    Several blank lines have been inserted at the top of the page.

3. Press the Alt-F6 keys.

    The cursor will align itself along the edge of the right margin.

4. Press Shift-F5.

    The Date menu will appear on the screen.

5. Type "3".

    The current date, entered flush against the right margin, is now on your screen.

    You have inserted a code in the document you will create. Now each time you retrieve this document, the current date (the one you enter when loading WordPerfect) will be displayed on the screen flush right.

    Name this document "Clarke.txt" when you save it.

What You Have Accomplished

You have embedded a code into **Clarke.txt** that displays and prints the current date each time this document is retrieved.   You have commanded the computer to place the date flush right.   It will be displayed in the default format.   This is a convenient way to handle form letters, because the date that is now on your screen will automatically be updated every time you retrieve or print this document.

✔ CHECKPOINT

a. Which keys access the Date menu?

_____

b. What is the default pattern for displaying the current date?

_____

INDENTING

As you create and edit your documents, you may want to set off a block of text by indenting it.   A paragraph can be indented just from the left margin or double indented from both the left and right margins.   In addition, a **hanging paragraph** can be created by starting the first line of the paragraph at the left margin and then indenting all of the remaining lines.

The Indent key (F4) lets you indent automatically without having to press the <TAB> key at the beginning of each line.   The Shift-F4 (Double Indent) keys let you indent from both margins automatically.   By pressing Shift-<TAB> after turning on the Indent, you can create a hanging paragraph. <CR> terminates the Indent feature.

GUIDED ACTIVITY: TYPING A PARAGRAPH

1.   Retrieve **Clarke.txt** if necessary.

2.   Press <CR> twice.

3.   Type the paragraph in Figure 7-3.

Arthur C. Clarke, a well-known science fiction writer, came up
with an observation on a phenomenon that has come to be known as
"Clarke's Law." It states that when a distinguished but elderly
scientist states that something is possible he is almost certainly
right. When he states that something is impossible he is very
probably wrong.

FIGURE 7-3   **Clarke.txt.**

GUIDED ACTIVITY: INDENTING TEXT FROM THE LEFT MARGIN

1.   Press <CR> three times.

2.   Press the F4 key.

    The Indent feature has been turned on.

3.   Type the paragraph in Figure 7-3 again.

4.   Press <CR>.

    The Indent feature has been turned off.

✔ CHECKPOINT

c.   Which key controls the Indent feature?

GUIDED ACTIVITY: INDENTING TEXT FROM THE RIGHT AND LEFT MARGINS

1.   Press <CR> twice.

2.   Press the Shift-F4 keys twice.

Double Indent has been turned on and your cursor has moved to the second tab stop.

3.   Type the paragraph in Figure 7-3 again.

4.   Press <CR>.

Double Indent has been turned off.

✔ CHECKPOINT

d.   How is the text on the screen formatted when the Shift-F4 keys are pressed?

GUIDED ACTIVITY: CREATING A HANGING PARAGRAPH

1.   Press <CR> twice.

2.   Press F4.

Indent has been turned on.

3.   Press Shift-<TAB> to move the first line of text one tab stop to the left.

4.   Type the paragraph in Figure 7-3 again.

The first line of the paragraph will be flush against the left margin. The remaining lines will be indented from the left margin.

5.   Press <CR> five times.

Indent has been turned off and several blank lines have been inserted at the bottom of the document.

✔ CHECKPOINT

e.   What two keystrokes are required to create a hanging paragraph?

_____

What You Have Accomplished

You have learned how to indent a paragraph from the left margin and how to double indent a paragraph. You have also learned the procedure for creating a "hanging" paragraph.   Indented paragraphs are used for long quotes or to emphasize particular elements within a long document. The choice of one of the three styles is a matter of personal preference.

REPEATING A CHARACTER OR FEATURE

Sometimes it is necessary to repeat a character several times when typing a document. By using the <ESC> (Escape) key, you can command the computer to repeat a specific alphabetic character, numeric character, or punctuation mark a specified number of times. The features that can be repeated by using the <ESC> key are included in the following list. The default number for the Repeat feature is eight. Therefore, unless you command the computer to do otherwise, a character or feature will automatically be repeated eight times.

Features That May Be Repeated:

1. Arrow keys.   The cursor moves a specified number of lines.

2. Delete word. A specified number of consecutive words are deleted.

3. Macro.   A macro is repeated a specified number of times.   Macros will be discussed in Unit 11.

4. Page Up/Down. The cursor scrolls up or down a specified number of pages.

5. Screen Up/Down.   The cursor scrolls up or down a specified number of screens.

6. Word Left/Right. The cursor moves a specified number of words either to the right or to the left.

GUIDED ACTIVITY: USING THE REPEAT FEATURE

1. Move the cursor to Ln 1, Pos 10, of Clarke.txt.

2. Press <ESC>.

    The Repeat feature has been turned on. The prompt "n=8" will appear in the status line.

3. Type "64".

    The feature or character you type next will be repeated sixty-four times.

4. Type "*" (asterisk).

    Sixty-four asterisks will appear on Ln 1 of your document.

5. Press <ESC> to turn on Repeat again.

    The prompt "n=8" will appear.

6. Type "50".

    The next feature or character you type will be repeated fifty times.

7. Press the <Down> arrow key.

    The cursor will move four lines past the last typed line of your document. It will not move down fifty lines because fifty lines have not been keyed in.

8. Press Shift-F6 to Center.

9. Press <ESC> to Repeat.

10. Type "30" after the prompt.

11. Type "*" (asterisk).

    Thirty asterisks will be centered on the last line of the document.

✔ CHECKPOINT

f. Which key do you press to activate Repeat?

_____

g. Identify the keystrokes required to repeat a character.

_____

What You Have Accomplished

You have used WordPerfect's Repeat feature to add asterisks across the top and bottom of your document, Clarke.txt.   You have also learned that the cursor will not move beyond the end of a document (the area you have typed in).

SUPERSCRIPTS AND SUBSCRIPTS

Some of the documents you create may require specialized typing functions.   For example, mathematical equations and chemical formulas usually require subscripts and superscripts.   Chemical symbols and foreign characters are also needed on occasion.   WordPerfect provides a Super/Subscript feature that will fill your specialized typing needs.   (Your printer must be capable of supporting them.)

When you press the Shift-F1 key, the Super/Subscript menu (Figure 7-4) appears on the screen.   This menu offers several options for specialized typing. You can select an option by typing one of the listed numbers.

1 Superscript; 2 Subscript; 3 Overstrike; 4 Adv Up; 5 Adv Dn; 6 Adv Ln: 0

FIGURE 7-4   Super/Subscript Menu.

The Super/Subscript menu options are defined as follows:

　　1 Superscript.   A character that is superscripted is placed 1/3 line above the other characters on the line.   The superscript is not displayed on your screen but will be printed.

　　2 Subscript.   A character that is subscripted is placed 1/3 line below the other characters on the line.   The subscript is not displayed on your screen but will be printed.

　　3 Overstrike.   This feature is used to print two characters in the same position.   It can be used to create chemical symbols and foreign characters.   Only the second character typed is visible on the screen, but both characters will be printed.

　　4 Adv Up.   A string of characters is printed 1/2 line above the other characters on the line.   The Ln number in the status line indicates which line the "advance up" characters will be printed on.

　　5 Adv Dn.   A string of characters is printed 1/2 line below the other characters on a line.   The Ln number in the status line indicates which line the "advance down" characters will be printed on.

6 **Adv Ln.**   This feature is an alternative to changing the top margin setting.   Blank lines are inserted as you command and text begins after the line insertions. The status line, however, continues to display the default setting.   This is a convenient feature to use for filling in forms because embedding an Advance Line code is more accurate than pressing <CR> to create blank lines.

GUIDED ACTIVITY: USING SUPERSCRIPTS

1. Retrieve **Clarke.txt** if necessary.

2. Move the cursor two lines below the last row of asterisks.

3. Type "The weather today is very warm.   The temperature is expected to reach 90".

4. Press Shift-F1.

The Super/Subscript menu will appear on the screen.

5. Type "1".

You have chosen Superscript from the menu.   An upper-case "S" will appear on the screen.

6. Type "o" (lower-case letter "o").

You have typed a superscript at the cursor location.   The "o" will appear on the screen in the normal position but will be superscripted when it is printed.

7. Press <SPACEBAR>.

8. Type "Fahrenheit.".

9. Press <CR> twice to leave two blank lines.

✔ CHECKPOINT

h.   Which keystrokes activate the Super/Subscript feature?

GUIDED ACTIVITY: USING SUBSCRIPTS

1. Type "The summation of several numbers could be indicated by the formula:".

2. Press the <SPACEBAR> five times.

3. Type "A".

4. Press the Shift-F1 keys.

    The Super/Subscript menu will appear on the screen.

5. Type "2".

    You have chosen Subscript from the menu. A lower-case "s" will appear in the status line.

6. Type "1".

7. Press <SPACEBAR>.

8. Type "+" (plus).

9. Press <SPACEBAR>.

10. Type "A".

11. Press the Shift-F1 keys.

12. Type "2".

13. Type "2".

    You have typed a subscript.

14. Press <SPACEBAR>.

15. Type "+" (plus).

16. Press <SPACEBAR>.

17. Type "A".

18. Press the Shift-F1 keys.

19. Type "2".

20. Type "3".

21. Press <SPACEBAR>.

22. Type "." (period) three times.

23. Press <SPACEBAR>.

24. Type "A".

25. Press the Shift-F1 keys.

26. Type "2".

27. Type "n" (lower-case letter "n")

28. Press <CR> twice to leave two blank lines.

✔ CHECKPOINT

   i. What prompt appears when you choose the Subscript option from the
       Super/Subscript menu?

_____

What You Have Accomplished

You have used the Super/Subscript menu to create a superscript and four
subscripts. Your screen displays the characters in a normal position but they
will be superscripted or subscripted if your printer supports these features.

GUIDED ACTIVITY: USING THE ADVANCE DOWN FEATURE

1. Type "The small child fell".

2. Press <SPACEBAR>.

3. Press the Shift-F1 keys.

    The Super/Subscript menu will appear on the screen.

4. Type "5".

    An arrow pointing down will appear on the screen. The status line will
    display a new line number.

5. Type "down".

6. Press <SPACEBAR>.

7. Press the Shift-F1 keys.

8. Type "5".

9. Type "down".

10. Press <SPACEBAR>.

11. Press the Shift-F1 keys.

12. Type "5".

13. Type "down.".

14. Save and Print **Clarke.txt**.

✔ CHECKPOINT

> j. What option from the Super/Subscript menu allows you to print a character 1/2 line down?

What You Have Accomplished

The **Clarke.txt** document that you have just created illustrates the Indent, Superscript, Subscript, and Advance Down features. It also contains the current date, flush right. If you followed the Guided Activities carefully, your printed document will look like that in Figure 7-5.

SEARCH AND REPLACE

Someday, after spending many hours creating a document, you may discover that you have repeatedly misspelled a word. Or you may decide that another word would better communicate your meaning. Maybe you would like to examine the document to verify that you did use a particular word correctly or that you did not neglect to mention someone's name. Instead of reading the document word by word, you can use WordPerfect's Search and Replace features to automatically find and replace words.

Search

You can search for both text and codes from any location within your document. A forward search will find any word or code you specify from the cursor forward through your document. A reverse search will find any word or code you specify from the cursor backward through your document. It is important to type the exact string of characters for which you are searching.

When you press F2, you will see the prompt "Srch:". Type the exact string of characters you want to find, then press F2 again. A forward search will begin. The cursor stops as soon as it finds the character string that you are seeking and waits for your decision. Each time you press F2, WordPerfect continues its search.

****

(today's date)

Arthur C. Clarke, a well-known science fiction writer, came up with an observation on a phenomenon that has come to be known as "Clarke's Law." It states that when a distinguished but elderly scientist states something is possible he is almost certainly right. When he states that something is impossible he is very probably wrong.

    Arthur C. Clarke, a well-known science fiction writer, came up with an observation on a phenomenon that has come to be known as "Clarke's Law." It states that when a distinguished but elderly scientist states something is possible he is almost certainly right. When he states that something is impossible he is very probably wrong.

        Arthur C. Clarke, a well-known science fiction writer, came up with an observation on a phenomenon that has come to be known as "Clarke's Law." It states that when a distinguished but elderly scientist states something is possible he is almost certainly right. When he states that something is impossible he is very probably wrong.

Arthur C. Clarke, a well-known science fiction writer, came up with an observation on a phenomenon that has come to be known as "Clarke's Law." It states that when a distinguished but elderly scientist states something is possible he is almost certainly right. When he states that something is impossible he is very probably wrong.

****

The weather today is very warm. The temperature is expected to reach 90° Fahrenheit.

The summation of several numbers could be indicated by the formula: $A_1 + A_2 + A_3 \ldots A_n$

The small child fell $_{down}$ $_{down}$ $_{down}$.

FIGURE 7-5 **Clarke.txt** (Revised).

If you would rather search backward, press the Shift-F2 keys for the same response in the reverse direction.

Replace

A word can be replaced automatically if you use the Search key in combination with the Replace key. You can either replace words automatically or approve each replacement individually. The Alt-F2 keys turn on the Replace feature. Type "Y" for automatic replacement or "N" for individual replacement. Then type the exact string of characters or code that you wish to replace and press F2. You will see the prompt "Replace with:". Type the new string of characters or codes, press F2, and begin searching and replacing.

Replace can be used only in a forward direction. Using both the Search and Replace features simultaneously to automatically replace words is referred to as a Global Search and Replace.

Hint: To find and replace whole words rather than character strings that may be a part of another word (e.g., "his" in "history"), enter spaces before and after the word to be replaced.

GUIDED ACTIVITY: SEARCHING UP AND DOWN

1. Retrieve the file **Wordperf.txt** from your WordPerfect Student Data disk.

2. Move the cursor to the first letter of the first word in **Wordperf.txt** to begin a forward search.

3. Press the F2 key.

    The prompt "Srch:" will appear in the status line.

4. Type "WP".   (Do **not** press <CR>.)

    You have identified a character string that WordPerfect will search for.

5. Press the F2 key.

    The Search has begun. The cursor will stop at the first occurrence of "WP".

6. Press the F2 key to continue the search.

    "Srch: WP" will appear on the screen.

7. Press the F2 key. The cursor will stop at the next occurrence of "WP".

8. Continue searching for "WP" by pressing the F2 key.

    When the Search has been completed, a "Not Found" message will appear briefly in the status line.

9. Move the cursor to the last letter of the last word in your document to begin a reverse search.

10. Press the Shift-F2 keys.

    The prompt "Srch:" will appear in the status line.

11. Type "PC" over "WP".

    You have identified a character string for which WordPerfect will search.

12. Press the Shift-F2 keys.

    The search has begun. The cursor will stop at the first occurrence of "PC".

13. Press the Shift-F2 keys to continue the Search.

    When the Search has been completed, a "Not Found" message will appear briefly in the status line.

✔ CHECKPOINT

k. Which keystroke is needed to search for a character string from the beginning to the end of a document?

_____

l. How will you know if the character string you are searching for does not occur in the part of the document that has been searched?

_____

m. Which keystrokes are needed to search in reverse?

_____

Hint: You can cancel the Search anytime by pressing the Cancel key (F1).

GUIDED ACTIVITY: AUTOMATIC SEARCH AND REPLACE

The Search and Replace feature works only in a forward direction.

1. Move the cursor to the first letter of the title of Wordperf.txt.

2. Press the Alt-F2 keys.

    The prompt "w/Confirm? (Y/N) N" will appear in the status line. If you type
    "Y", the cursor will stop at each occurrence of the designated character
    string and let you confirm its replacement. If you type "N" (the default),
    all designated character strings will automatically be replaced.

3. Type "N".

    You have commanded the program to automatically replace the designated
    character string. The prompt "Srch:" will appear in the status line.

4. Type "WP".

    You have identified a character string for which WordPerfect will search.

5. Press the F2 key.

    The prompt "Replace with:" will appear in the status line.

6. Type "WordPerfect".

    You have identified a character string that will replace the character string
    "WP".

7. Press the F2 key.

    Search and Replace has begun.   "WP" will automatically be replaced with
    "WordPerfect".

8. Save and Print Wordperf.txt.

    The printed document will look like that in Figure 7-6.

✔ CHECKPOINT

    n. What keystrokes are required to automatically replace a character string?

WordPerfect CORPORATION

<u>Business Acquisition.</u>

In business, the smart money is spent in areas that improve the bottom line. Areas like productivity and efficiency. That's why a lot of companies today are investing their money in WordPerfect 4.1 for powerful business word processing.

Substantial dividends.

With unsurpassed business features for the IBM PC and compatibles, WordPerfect 4.1 pays for itself again and again with professional documents turned out in record time. Features include an elegant thesaurus, 115,000-word spelling dictionary, columns displayed side-by-side on screen, math capabilities, split screen, and line drawing.

In addition, WordPerfect Corporation offers an excellent site licensing program so major customers can receive the software and support they need for a pre-determined, discounted fee.

The top seller.

With so much to offer, WordPerfect has now become the best-selling word processor for the IBM PC, according to market research firm Info-Corp. And customers like Merrill Lynch, Upjohn and General Dynamics are leading the way.

Maximize your investment.

Get the word processor designed to improve your company's bottom line. WordPerfect 4.1. It's the perfect corporate investment. For more information, call or write WordPerfect Corp., 288 West Center St., Orem, Utah 84057, (801) 227-4000.

FIGURE 7-6   **Wordperf.txt.**

FOOTNOTES AND ENDNOTES

Footnotes and endnotes are notes of reference, explanation or comment placed outside regular text on a printed page. Footnotes are placed at the bottom of a referenced page. Endnotes are compiled and placed at the end of a document.

WordPerfect automatically numbers footnotes and endnotes and arranges them on a printed page. The text of a footnote or endnote can be up to 16,000 lines long, and can be edited just like normal text. An Options selection on the Footnote menu lets you change the formatting of the footnote or endnote.

The Footnote Menu

When you press Ctrl-F7, the Footnote menu (Figure 7-7) appears. You can select an option by typing one of the listed numbers.

1 Create; 2 Edit; 3 New #; 4 Options; 5 Create Endnote; 6 Edit Endnote: 0

FIGURE 7-7   Footnote Menu.

The options on this menu are defined as follows:

  1 Create. Select this option to create a footnote. A blank screen appears along with the number of the current footnote. The status line on this screen displays the current position and line number of the cursor.

  2 Edit. Select this option to edit a footnote. The message "Ftn#?" appears in the status line. Type the number of the footnote you wish to edit.

  3 New #. The prompt "Ftn#?" appears in the status line. Use this option when you want footnote numbering to start at a particular number. For example, you may wish to start footnote numbering over again at the beginning of each chapter in a book.

  4 Options. The Footnote Options submenu appears. Use this submenu to change the format of your footnotes.

  5 Create Endnote. Select this option to create an endnote. A blank screen appears along with the number of the current endnote.

  6 Edit Endnote. Select this option to edit an endnote. The message "Endn#?" appears in the status line. Type the number of the endnote you wish to edit.

GUIDED ACTIVITY: CREATING FOOTNOTES

1. Retrieve Educate.txt from your WordPerfect Student Data disk.

2. Move the cursor to the second page of the document, under the heading "Forces of Change" and after the words "basic skills" at the end of the second paragraph.

3. Press the Ctrl-F7 keys.

    The Footnote menu appears on your screen.

4. Type "1".

    A blank screen will appear. The status line on this screen will display the current Pos and Ln number of the cursor.

5. Type the following text:

    "National Commission on Excellence in Education, <u>A Nation at Risk: The Imperative for Educational Reform,</u> Washington, D.C., Government Printing Office, 1983, pp. 7-8."

    Your first footnote has been created. WordPerfect will save enough lines at the bottom of the page of text so that the footnote can be printed.

6. Press the F7 key.

    Educate.txt will reappear on your screen.

7. Move the cursor to the end of the next paragraph. The paragraph ends with the words "and a satisfying life."

8. Press the Ctrl-F7 keys.

9. Type "1" to create a second footnote.

10. Type the following text on the editing screen:

    "Ibid, p. 17."

11. Press the F7 key.

    Educate.txt will reappear on your screen.

12. Move the cursor to the third page of the document and to the end of the second sentence in the first paragraph under the heading "Threats". This sentence ends with the words "academically able students.".

13. Press the Ctrl-F7 keys.

14. Type "1" to create a third footnote.

15. Type the following text on the editing screen:

    "Ibid, p. 22-23."

16. Press the F7 key.

    Educate.txt will reappear on your screen.

20. Save and Print Educate.txt.

THE TAB RULER

The Tab Ruler displays the tab and margin settings that are being used in the document you are currently editing. Each triangle in the Tab Ruler indicates a tab setting. Each bracket indicates a margin setting. A brace is used to indicate that a tab and margin setting are in the same position. If the document you are editing contains a number of different tab or margin settings, the Tab Ruler changes to reflect the settings at the cursor location.

A Tab Ruler is usually used to split a screen into two windows so that you can edit two documents at the same time. However, you may also display the Tab Ruler to edit a single document.

The <Up> and <Down> cursor movement keys are used to adjust the position of the Tab Ruler. <CR> is used to anchor the Tab Ruler in place.

When you press the Ctrl-F3 keys, the Screen menu (Figure 7-1) appears. Select option 1 to access the Tab Ruler or to split the screen into two windows.

0 Rewrite; 1 Window; 2 Line Draw; 3 Ctrl/Alt keys; 4 Colors; 5 Auto Rewrite:0

FIGURE 7-1 Screen Menu.

The Window option is defined as follows:

1 Window. This option is used to split your screen so that you can edit two documents at the same time. The prompt "# Lines in this Window" appears. If you plan to split screens, respond to the prompt by typing the number of lines you need to display your current document. The remaining lines are used to display the second document you will edit.

If you want the Tab Ruler to appear but do not want to split screens, answer the prompt "# Lines in this Window" by using the <Down> arrow key to move the Tab Ruler to the bottom of your screen. Then press <CR> to anchor it in place.

When you want to delete the Tab Ruler, press Ctrl-F3 again, type "1", then type any number equal to or greater than 24 (the number of lines on a screen).

GUIDED ACTIVITY: DISPLAYING THE TAB RULER

1. Retrieve **Olson.ltr.**

2. Press the Ctrl-F3 keys.

    The Screen menu will appear on your screen.

3. Type "1".

    The prompt "# Lines in this Window:" will appear.

4. Type "8".

    The Tab Ruler will be anchored on Ln 9 of your screen.

5. Press <CR>.

    The Tab Ruler has been anchored.

6. Press Shift-F8 to access the Line Format menu. Change the tab settings. Notice that the Tab setting indicators on the Tab Ruler have changed to reflect the new tab settings.

7. Use the cursor movement keys to scroll back the lines of your document. Watch the Tab Ruler change to reflect the tab settings at the cursor position.

8. Press the Ctrl-F3 keys.

    The Screen menu will appear on your screen.

9. Type "1".

The prompt "# Lines in this Window:" will appear.

10. Type "30".

Any number of lines greater than the number of lines on a screen (i.e., 24) will remove the Tab Ruler.

11. Press <CR>.

The window is closed.

✔ CHECKPOINT

o. Which keystrokes are needed to display the Tab Ruler?

_____

p. How is Tab Ruler removed from the screen?

_____

SPLIT SCREEN

When you split the screen to create two windows, you can edit two documents at the same time. Each document appears in a separate window with its own status line. The Tab Ruler is used to separate the two windows. When your cursor is positioned in the upper window, the triangles on the Tab Ruler point up. When the cursor is in the lower window, the triangles point down.

Select the window option on the Screen menu to split your screen. Answer the prompt by typing the number of lines you need to display your first document in the upper window. The default setting is 24, which is the total number of lines on the screen. Therefore, if you select 24, you will not really have a split screen because you will not be able to see two documents at the same time. Since a window must contain at least two lines, type "22" or less after the prompt for a true split screen.

Press the Switch key (Shift-F3) to move the cursor between windows. Each window is controlled separately, so any functions you activate affect only the document in which your cursor is located. Be sure that you Exit both documents before you Exit WordPerfect.

REVIEW QUESTIONS

1. Suppose that your company sends a form letter repeatedly during the course of the month. How would you format that letter to avoid changing the date each time you send it?

2. Suppose the form letter you send out requires you to insert the current date within the body of the text. How would you go about accomplishing this task?

3. Which keys would you use to insert a string of twenty asterisks on a page of a document?

4. You have come upon a rather long quote from a renowned scientist and decide that it is just what you need to make a point in the proposal you are writing.   Which keystrokes will most quickly and efficiently set the paragraph in one tab stop from the right and left margins?

5. Which keystrokes must you use to create a hanging paragraph?

6. Identify the keys that access the Date menu.

7. What is the default number for the Repeat feature?

8. How can you use the Repeat feature to scroll a document up eight pages? up ten pages?

9. Which keys are needed to delete eight consecutive words?

10. Suppose that you have just finished typing a long document and it occurs to you that you should have typed "chairperson" instead of "chairman." How can you quickly replace each incorrect word with the correct one?

_____

11. Define the term "default."

_____

12. Identify the keys that access the Super/Subscript menu.

_____

13. You have just finished writing a proposal and have a nagging suspicion that you have overused the word "collaborate." How can you quickly examine your document and selectively replace the word?

_____

14. What is the Overstrike option on the Super/Subscript menu used for?

_____

15. How will characters be printed when you use the Superscript option on the Super/Subscript menu?

_____

16. Explain how to anchor the Tab Ruler at the bottom of your screen when you wish to use it to edit a single document.

_____

DOCUMENTATION RESEARCH

1. Suppose that you wish to use the Indent feature to indent a paragraph twelve spaces. How do you change the indent value of the indent key?

_____

2. Using the Date and Time feature, select a format for displaying the date and time. What is the maximum number of characters that can be used in a format pattern?

_____

3.   How is the Replace feature used to find whole words (e.g., **not,** instead of **cannot** or **another**)?

_____

4.   If you type all upper-case letters to search for a specific word, how will the WordPerfect program respond?

_____

5.   List the WordPerfect features that can be used in a replace string.

_____

6.   Use the Reference section to learn how to use the Overstrike feature to print two characters in the same position. Retrieve a document and try it.

_____

8

FILE MANAGEMENT

SUPPLIES NEEDED

1. WordPerfect program disk
2. WordPerfect Student Data disks

OBJECTIVES

After completing this unit, you will be able to use the list files to

1. list all files in a directory;
2. retrieve a file;
3. delete a file;
4. rename a file;
5. print a file;
6. copy a file.

IMPORTANT KEYSTROKES

1. F5..................................to list files
2. Ctrl-F5...........................to lock a document

ASSIGNMENTS

1. Retrieve Forfun
2. Print Olson.ltr
3. Rename Dummy
4. Delete Smart
5. Review Questions
6. Research Documentation

FILE MANAGEMENT

You have by now created a number of documents and stored them on specific files on your WordPerfect Student Data disk. You gave each of your files a meaningful name to make it easier to remember which document you stored in a specific file. As your store of documents increases, it becomes less practical for you to remember all of the documents you have created. This is when WordPerfect's List Files feature (F5) is valuable. It helps you organize your files so that they can be easily retrieved, printed, copied, renamed, or even erased.

Your data storage disk is much like the filing cabinet in a traditional office. Both are used to store units of information on "files." When information is needed, the file is opened, read, revised, and then closed.

The operating system (DOS) maintains a directory of the files you have stored. When you press F5 (List Files), the name of the default drive and/or directory appears on the status line. If you press <CR>, the directory, a list of files in alphabetical order, appears on the screen along with the List Files menu (Figure 8-1). To see the files in another directory on another disk, change the drive designation (e.g., A: B:).

A sample directory is included in Figure 8-1. The header displays the directory name, the current date, and the time of day. It also informs you how much storage space (in bytes) is left on your data disk and how much storage space the document you are working on takes up (in bytes).   For each filename listed, its size (in bytes) and the date and time it was last edited and saved is included.

Select a file you wish to open by highlighting it with the cursor movement keys. Then select an option from the List Files menu by typing one of the listed numbers.

```
08/21/86  02:46              Directory B:\*.*
Document Size:        7218                    Free Disk Space:      247808

. <CURRENT>   <DIR>
CHKPT    .WRP    3527  08/19/86 18:02   3   COLUMNS .WRP    4827  08/19/86  09:02
CONTENTS.WRP    6483  08/20/86 13:22   3   INTRO   .WRP    8146  08/18/86  21:21
MACROS   .WRP   11339  08/17/86 14:21   3   MATH    .WRP   13352  08/18/86  14:11
MGMT     .WRP    7267  08/19/86 09:45   3   PREAMBLE.        249  08/16/86  18:55
RESEARCH.WRP    4920  08/19/86 16.33   3   RULER   .WRP    9985  08/20/86  18:11
UNIT9    .WRP   18966  08/19/86 10:25   3   WRDPERF .TXT   19456  07/26/86  15:33




1 Retrieve; 2 Delete; 3 Rename; 4 Print; 5 Text In;
6 Look; 7 Change Directory; 8 Copy; 9 Word Search: 0
```

FIGURE 8-1   List Files Menu and Sample Directory.

The options on the List Files menu are defined as follows:

1 Retrieve. A copy of the file highlighted by the cursor is retrieved and placed on the screen. If you are editing another document when you press F5, the retrieved document is inserted where the cursor was resting. Text below the cursor is pushed down to make room for the retrieved document. Make sure you clear your screen before retrieving a document unless you intend to append a file. Use this option when you do not remember the name of the file you wish to retrieve or when you need information from a file that you are not currently working on.

2 Delete. The prompt "Delete filename? Y/N N" appears on the screen. Type "Y" to erase (delete) the file. Press any other key if you change your mind and decide to keep the file after all. Be careful. Once a file is erased it cannot be restored.

3 Rename. The prompt "New Name" appears at the bottom of your screen. Choose this option and give your file a new name. Renaming files may be necessary as your store increases and you need to reorganize.

4 Print. The highlighted file is sent directly to the printer. This saves time when you want to print a document that does not need editing.

5 Text In. A copy of a file created with a program other than WordPerfect and stored on your data disk can be retrieved and placed on the screen. An ASCII format file must be created to translate the file. Refer to your WordPerfect manual for an explanation of this procedure.

6 Look. This option lets you examine, but not edit, the contents of a file. It also lets you view the filenames in another directory.

7 Change Directory. The prompt "New Directory = 'current directory'" appears on the screen. Type the name of the new directory you wish to create. The prompt "Create New Directory Y/N N" will appear. Type "Y" and a new directory is created.

8 Copy. A copy of the highlighted file can be placed on another file, in another directory, or on another disk.

9 Word Search. The prompt "Word Pattern:" appears on the screen. With this option, you can search for files that contain a particular word, phrase, or word pattern. Use the ? and * to denote missing characters in a word pattern, and enclose all words and word patterns in double quotation marks. For example, "letter" will select all files that contain the word "letter" and "l?ne" will select all the files that contain words that match this word pattern (e.g., "line", "lone", "lane").

GUIDED ACTIVITY: USING LIST FILES TO RETRIEVE A DOCUMENT

1. Display a clear screen and be sure your "WordPerfect Student Data" disk is in Drive B.

2. Press the F5 key to activate the List Files function.

    A message showing the default directory will appear on the screen.

3. Press <CR>.

    The directory of your WordPerfect Student Data disk will appear on the screen.

4. Highlight the file **Forfun**.

5. Type "1" to Retrieve the file.

    Forfun will appear on the screen.

GUIDED ACTIVITY: USING LIST FILES TO PRINT A DOCUMENT

1. Display a clear screen.

2. Press the F5 key, then <CR>, for List Files.

    The directory of your WordPerfect Student Data disk will appear on the screen.

3. Highlight the file Olson.ltr.

4. Type "4" to Print the file.

   Olson.ltr will be printed without being retrieved.

GUIDED ACTIVITY: USING LIST FILES TO LOOK AT A FILE

1. Highlight the file Dummy.

2. Type "3" to activate the Look option.

   The file Dummy will appear on the screen.

3. Press any key to return to the list of files.

GUIDED ACTIVITY: USING LIST FILES TO RENAME A FILE

1. Highlight the file Dummy.

2. Type "3" to Rename the file.

   The prompt "New Name:" will appear at the bottom of your screen.

3. Type "Smart".

4. Press <CR>.

   The file Dummy has been renamed Smart.

GUIDED ACTIVITY: USING LIST FILES TO DELETE A FILE

1. Highlight the file Smart.

2. Type "2" to Delete the file.

   The prompt "Delete B:\SMART?(Y/N) N" will appear at the bottom of your screen.

3. Type "Y".

   The file Smart will be erased and will no longer be listed.

LOCKED DOCUMENTS

If you need to protect or "lock" a document, you can do so by inserting a secret password. This password must then be entered before a document can be retrieved or printed.

This feature may be convenient for those documents that require top security, but do not use it indiscriminately. Once you lock a document, you cannot retrieve it except with your password--and secret passwords are easy to forget.

To lock a document, press the Ctrl-F5 keys to access the Text In/Text Out menu. Select option 3, then type your secret password. You will be prompted to enter the password again. This is the program's way of guarding against typing errors. The password will not appear on the screen.

After entering your secret password, you will be prompted to enter the name of the file you are locking.

To retrieve a locked document, press Shift-F10 to Retrieve or F5 for the list of files. You will be prompted to enter your secret password.

If you lock a document and then decide that the document is more secure unlocked, press Ctrl-F5 and select option 4. You will first be prompted to enter the name of your document, and then to enter your secret password. If you enter the password incorrectly, the message "File is locked" appears on your screen. If you cannot recall your secret password, you will never see your document again.

REVIEW QUESTIONS

1. What is the purpose of a directory?

    _____

2. Identify each of the components contained in the header of a directory.

    _____

3. The List Files menu contains nine options. Which option lets you retrieve a file to edit?

    _____

4. How is a file selected from a directory on the List Files screen?

    _____

5. Suppose that you want to retrieve a particular file in a large directory but cannot remember the exact filename. How can you most efficiently examine the contents of a file without first retrieving it?

6. Suppose that you would like to erase some outdated files from your data storage disk. How would you do so?

7. Suppose that you are writing a novel. You store each chapter in a separate file, named by chapter (e.g., **Chap1.nov**). By the time you get to your tenth chapter, you have already made extensive revisions and even inserted new chapters. You realize that your system of naming files is no longer practical. How will you reorganize?

8. Why should the Locked Document feature be used with caution?

DOCUMENTATION RESEARCH

1. What is WordPerfect's prerequisite for deleting a directory?

2. How is the list of files affected when you type "N" in response to the prompt "Replace filename (Y/N) Y" as you Exit WordPerfect?

3. Suppose that your default drive is A. You would like to see the directory of files stored on the disk in Drive B. Describe how this can be done.

4. The directory lists each file by its filename and its size in bytes. Use the glossary to find the meaning of "byte."

5. Suppose that, after you attempt to Retrieve a file, the message "Error:File not found" appears on the screen. Give three reasons why this may happen.

APPLICATION

C

SUPPLIES NEEDED

1. WordPerfect program disk
2. WordPerfect Learning disk
3. WordPerfect Student Data disk
4. printer

ASSIGNMENTS

The assignments to be completed for this Application section are

1. Create **Cleanup.ltr**
2. Create **Business.txt**
3. Create **Micro.txt**
4. Create **Printer.txt**
5. Print multiple copies of a file
6. Queue print jobs

APPLICATIONS

This Application section contains a number of documents that can be reproduced to apply the skills you have acquired in Units 1 through 8. Format your documents so that they look like the ones on the printed pages of this section. Some format instructions have been handwritten on the pages of this section to guide you.

Use your template and the Quick Reference card to find the keystroke commands and **menus you need.** Remember that there is often more than one keystroke choice that can be used to create and format a document. Your primary task is to find the most efficient way to reproduce the documents.

You may also wish to experiment with naming and renaming files, or with copying and deleting files. The more adept you become at managing your files, the easier and more productive your word-processing tasks will become.

You may also want to create your own applications—some tasks that are more meaningful to your everyday work. Your WordPerfect Student Data disk should have plenty of space available (use List Files to find out how much) to store additional documents.

Name this document Cleanup.ltr

10 pitch
left margin 10
right margin 74

(current date)
flush right

<u>LAKEWOOD SCHOOL</u>
<u>LAND DEVELOPMENT COMMITTEE</u>

Dear Members of the Land Development Committee:

We need your help as we continue our work on our nature trail and camping area in the wooded lots at our school.

                 SATURDAY, APRIL 20TH AT 8:30 A.M.

double indent twice

On this day, we will finish clearing the nature trail and camping area and we will chip the cut-down tree branches and spread the chips on the nature trail and camping area.   (We have rented a mechanical chipper.)

Bring: Chain saws, wheelbarrows, sprayers, rakes, and gloves.

                 SATURDAY, APRIL 27TH AT 8:30 A.M.

double indent twice

On this day we will plant the trees (seedlings) that we have obtained.

Bring: Planting bars, shovels, wheelbarrows, buckets, and gloves.

We need lots of manpower and womanpower for this work. Recruit and bring a friend if you can.

Enthusiasm on this committee is running very high. Let's keep up the momentum. This project will provide a wonderful nature appreciation and camping experience for our youth -- and it will beautify our school property! This is one of our Top Priority projects.

Glenn Maki   Jim Johnson, Principal

Type the quotation and sentence as shown then use the Search and Replace feature to make them more meaningful.

Call on a b man at b times only, and on b, transact your b and go about your b, in order to give him time to finish his b.   WELLINGTON

Replace b with the word "business".

Name this document Business.txt

Some computer labs use IBM PC,s while others use Z or C PC equipment.   There are many other brands of micros that are also IBM compatible.

Replace "IBM" with "International Business Machines"
      "PC's" with "Personal Computer equipment"
      "C"   with "Compac"
      "micros" with "microcomputers"
      "Z" with "Zenith"

Name this document Micro.txt

Type the sentence six times using the formatting directions given under each example.

It is necessary to try to surpass one's self always; this occupation ought to last as long as life. Queen Christina

Pitch: 10; Margins: 10, 74

It is necessary to try to surpass one's self always; this occupation ought to last as long as life. Queen Christina

Pitch: 12; Margins: 12, 86

It is necessary to try to surpass one's self always; this occupation ought to last as long as life. Queen Christina

Pitch: 10; Margins: 10, 74; Tabs: Every 5 spaces; Indent from right margin

It is necessary to try to surpass one's self always; this occupation ought to last as long as life. Queen Christina

Pitch 10; Margins: 10, 74; Tabs: Every 5 spaces; Indent from both right and left margins

It is necessary to try to surpass one's self always; this occupation ought to last as long as life. Queen Christina

Pitch 12; Margins: 12, 93; Tabs: Every 6 spaces; Indent from both right and left margins twice

It is necessary to try to surpass one's self always; this occupation ought to last as long as life. Queen Christina

Pitch 12; Margins: 12, 93; Tabs: Every 6 spaces; Right justification off

Name this document Printer.tyt

Use the Print function to print 2 copies of **Printer.txt**.

Use the Print function to queue up three print jobs; **Cleanup.ltr**, **Business.txt** and **Printer.txt**. Print all three jobs.

2 SPECIAL FEATURES

UNIT

9

SPELLER AND THESAURUS

SUPPLIES NEEDED

1. WordPerfect program disk
2. WordPerfect Speller disk
3. WordPerfect Thesaurus disk
4. WordPerfect Student Data disk
5. printer

OBJECTIVES

After completing this unit, you will be able to

1. correct spelling errors with the WordPerfect Speller;
2. add and delete words from the dictionary;
3. count the number of words on a page;
4. select synonyms with the WordPerfect Thesaurus.

IMPORTANT KEYSTROKES

1. Ctrl-F2......................to use the Speller
2. Alt-F1......................to use the Thesaurus

ASSIGNMENTS

1. Edit Preamble
2. Review Questions
3. Research Documentation

THE SPELLER

Proofreading is a critical part of editing a document. It is up to you to check your document for meaning and word usage. However, the WordPerfect Speller can save you proofreading time by checking for spelling errors.

The WordPerfect Speller contains a dictionary of over 100,000 words. It is made up of a main word list and a common word list. You may also maintain a supplementary dictionary file of words that are not included in the main dictionary.

The WordPerfect Speller program compares the words in a document to the list of correctly spelled words in the dictionary. With the Speller, you can check an entire document, a single page, or an individual word. You can also check words phonetically or according to a pattern. Therefore, even when you can only get close to the spelling of a word, the WordPerfect Speller can find the correct spelling.

The WordPerfect Speller program is stored on a separate disk. Therefore the document you wish to spell-check must first be retrieved; then your Student Data disk must be removed from Drive B and replaced with the Speller disk. If you are using a hard disk system, first retrieve the document you wish to check, then start the Speller.

THE CHECK MENU

When you press Ctrl-F2, the Speller is started and the Check menu (Figure 9-1) appears on the screen. You can select an option from this menu by typing one of the listed numbers.

Check: 1 Word; 2 Page; 3 Document; 4 Change Dictionary; 5 Look Up; 6 Count

FIGURE 9-1   Check Menu.

The Check menu options are defined as follows:

1 Word.   The word on which your cursor is located is checked for spelling errors. If the word is spelled correctly, the cursor jumps to the next word. If the word is not spelled correctly (that is, not found in the dictionary), it is highlighted and a Not Found submenu appears along with a list of possible replacement words. You can either choose the word with the correct spelling or choose one of the submenu options.

2 Page.   The page on which your cursor is located is checked for spelling errors. The Speller starts its spell-check at the beginning of the page. Each word not spelled correctly (that is, not found in the dictionary) is highlighted and the Not Found submenu appears on the screen along with a list of possible replacement words. You can either choose the word with the correct spelling or select a submenu option.

3 Document.   The entire document is spell-checked from beginning to end. A "Please wait" message appears at the bottom of the screen until the Speller finds a misspelling.

When the Speller is finished, the total number of words checked appears at the bottom of the screen.

Anytime you wish to stop a spell-check, press the Cancel key (F1).

4 Change Dictionary.   When you choose this option, you can switch from the main dictionary to a supplementary or user-created dictionary. The Speller Utility program on the Speller disk can help you to create a new dictionary when the vocabulary you use is specialized (for example, legal or medical terms).

5 Look Up.   A "Word Pattern" prompt appears on your screen. A word pattern can be created using a ? for each letter questioned or an * for successive missing letters. The Speller matches the pattern to words contained in the dictionary and displays a list of possible replacement words. For example, you can find the correct spelling for the word "aristocratic" by typing aris*rat*, and for "blatant" by typing "blat?nt".

6 Count.   The words in your document are counted and the word count is displayed at the bottom of your screen.

THE NOT FOUND SUBMENU

Each time the WordPerfect Speller finds a misspelled word in the document you are spell-checking, the word is highlighted and the Not Found submenu
(Figure 9-2) appears on your screen. From this submenu, you can either select a replacement word or choose a submenu option. You may select an option by typing one of the listed numbers.

```
Not Found!  Select Word or Menu Option (0=Continue): 0
1 Skip Once; 2 Skip; 3 Add Word; 4 Edit; 5 Look Up; 6 Phonetic:0
```

FIGURE 9-2   Not Found Submenu.

1 Skip Once. If you choose this option, the highlighted word is skipped over and the spell-check continues. The next time the skipped word appears in your document, it is again highlighted.

2 Skip. If you choose this option, the highlighted word is skipped over and the spell-check continues. If the skipped word appears again in your document, it is ignored.

3 Add Word. The highlighted word is added to the supplementary dictionary and the spell-check continues. You can add the supplementary dictionary to the main dictionary by using the Speller Utility program on the Speller disk.

4 Edit. When you choose this option, the cursor jumps to the highlighted word and you can make a correction yourself. Then press <CR> and the spell-check continues.

5 Look Up. A "Word Pattern" prompt is displayed on your screen. You can create a pattern using ? or * for missing characters. This option is also available on the Check menu.

6 Phonetic. All the words in the dictionary that sound like the word not found are displayed.

THE DOUBLE WORD SUBMENU

If the Speller finds a duplicate word (the same word typed twice in succession), the Double Word submenu (Figure 9-3) appears on your screen.

```
Double Word!   1 2 Skip; 3 Delete 2nd; 4 Edit; 5 Disable double word checking
```

FIGURE 9-3   Double Word Submenu.

This submenu contains five options, defined as follows:

1 2 Skip. The highlighted double words are skipped over and the spell-check will continues.

3 Delete 2nd. The second occurrence of the word is deleted.

4 Edit. The cursor jumps to the highlighted words; you edit these as desired.

5 Disable double word checking. If you prefer not to check double word occurrences, use this option to disable the feature.

GUIDED ACTIVITY: SPELL-CHECKING

Always make certain that your document has been saved on your data storage disk before loading the WordPerfect Speller.

1. Retrieve **Preamble** from your Wordperfect Student Data disk. Remove this disk from Drive B.

2. Insert the WordPerfect Speller disk into Drive B.

3. Move the cursor to the beginning of the **Preamble** document.

4. Press the Ctrl-F2 keys.

   The Check menu will appear on the screen.

5. Type "2" to spell-check the page.

   The first set of double words will be highlighted.

6. Type "3" to delete the second occurrence.

7. The spell-check will continue. The next misspelled word will be highlighted and a list of replacement words will appear.

8. Type the letter in front of the correct spelling. The highlighted word will be replaced and the spell-check will continue.

9. Continue to spell-check the page. After the spell-check has been completed, the number of words checked will appear at the bottom of your screen.

✔ CHECKPOINT

a. How many words were spell-checked?

10.   Remove the Speller disk and replace it with your WordPerfect Student Data
      disk.

11.   Save **Preamble**.

What You Have Accomplished

You have loaded the Speller program and used it to spell-check a short document.
The Speller found misspelled words as well as double word occurrences. You have
now proofread your document for spelling errors.

THE THESAURUS

The WordPerfect Thesaurus helps you choose exactly the right words as you create
your documents.   It displays a list of nouns, verbs, and adjectives that are
similar in meaning to a word you might want to revise. You can either direct the
Thesaurus to automatically replace a word or to keep the word you originally
typed.

Like the WordPerfect Speller, the WordPerfect Thesaurus is stored on a separate
disk.   To use the Thesaurus, remove your data disk from Drive B and insert the
Thesaurus disk.   When you are finished with the Thesaurus, return your data disk
to Drive B so that you can save your files.

When you want to use the Thesaurus, move the cursor to the word you would like to
revise and press the Alt-F1 keys. The Thesaurus menu and a sample screen (Figure
9-4) will appear on your screen.   The upper part of your screen displays four
lines of your document.   The lower part of your screen is divided into three
columns, each containing subgroups of reference words. Use the arrow keys to move
through the columns.

```
information (n)

1 A .data
  B .detail
  C  facts
  D .intelligence
  E .knowledge
  F .material
  G .news


1 Replace Word; 2 View Doc; 3 Look Up Word; 4 Clear Column: 0
```

FIGURE 9-4   Thesaurus Menu and Sample Screen.

The Thesaurus menu contains four options that allow you to look up words in four different ways. The options are defined as follows:

1 Replace Word. The prompt "Press letter for word" appears. You may select a word from the displayed list of replacement choices by typing the letter printed in front of the word.

2 View Doc. Use this option to place your cursor back into the document. Press the Exit key to return to the Thesaurus. This option may also be used when you wish to see more text before choosing a replacement word.

3 Look Up Word. The prompt "Word" appears. With this option you can look up a word that does not appear in the document. Type the word you want to look up, and a list of words with similar meanings appears on the screen.

4 Clear Column. The list of replacement words can be cleared one column at a time to make room for additional words you need to look up.

To exit the Thesaurus, press <CR>, <SPACEBAR>, or F7.

The WordPerfect Thesaurus makes use of three special terms to guide you in your quest for the perfect word. These terms are defined as follows:

1 Headword. A headword is a word that can be looked up in the Thesaurus. If you see the message "Not a Headword", it means that the word you want to look up is not listed.

2 Reference. A reference word is a word that is similar in meaning to the headword. Reference words are displayed in columns under the headword. References that are preceded by bullets (.) are also headwords and can be looked up separately.

3 Subgroups. Subgroups are groups of reference words with the same connotation. They are arranged in numbered groups under the headword.

Hint: To avoid swapping disks each time you want to use the Thesaurus, copy the Thesaurus files (TH.WP) to your data disk. Refer to Appendix A for instructions on copying files.

GUIDED ACTIVITY: USING THE THESAURUS

In this activity you use the WordPerfect Thesaurus to restore the Preamble to the United States Constitution. If you must, look up the Preamble to determine if you have restored it correctly.

1. Retrieve **Preamble** if necessary and move the cursor to the beginning of the document.

2. Replace your WordPerfect Student Data disk with the Thesaurus disk.

3. Place the cursor on the first incorrect word in Preamble.

4. Press the Alt-F1 keys.

    A list of words will appear on the screen. Choose the correct replacement word.

5. Find the next incorrect word in Preamble.

6. Press the Alt-F1 keys.

    A list of words will appear on the screen. Choose the correct replacement word.

7. Continue using the Thesaurus to replace words in this document until you have restored the Preamble to its authentic version.

✔ CHECKPOINT

b. Which option do you choose from the Thesaurus menu to replace a word in a document?

_____

REVIEW QUESTIONS

1. Assume that you have typed a document and are ready to spell-check it. Which option from the Check menu do you choose?

_____

2. Explain what happens when the WordPerfect Speller finds a misspelled word.

_____

3. Suppose that you work for a pharmaceutical firm that makes frequent use of medical terms. How can you set up the WordPerfect Speller so that these specialized terms can be looked up?

_____

4. Imagine that you are a highly skilled project manager but a terrible speller. Because of this limitation, the reports you write take a great deal of time and effort. How can you use the WordPerfect Speller to correctly spell the words you are only capable of guessing at?

_____

5. Imagine that you are a freelance writer and are paid by the word. How can you use the WordPerfect Speller to determine quickly how many words are contained in your manuscript?

   ==

6. How can you cancel a spell-check?

   ==

7. Explain what happens when the Speller checks the following sentence:

   "At times you you will make a typing error."

   How can you delete one of the "you"s?

   ==

8. Suppose that as the Speller checks your document, it highlights many specialized words that are correctly spelled but are not found in the main dictionary. How can you add these words to the dictionary so that the next time you want to spell-check your documents these specialized words will be found?

   ==

9. Both the WordPerfect Speller and the WordPerfect Thesaurus are stored on separate disks. Explain how to load each of these programs on a dual drive computer system.

   ==

10. What does the term "headword" mean in the Thesaurus program?

    ==

11. The meaning of a word depends on the context in which it is used. How does the Thesaurus allow you to consider context before making word-replacement decisions?

    ==

12. Suppose that you place your cursor on a word and access the Thesaurus to look up its meaning. You then decide that the word does not communicate what you mean. How can you use the Thesaurus to investigate the meaning of another word you are considering?

    ==

DOCUMENTATION RESEARCH

1. How does the Speller program handle the words you have instructed it to skip during a spell-check?

    ───

2. What is the Speller Utility program on the Speller disk used for?

    ───

3. Define the purpose of each option available on the Speller Utility menu.

    ───

4. Use the Speller/Thesaurus section of the user's manual to find out how the cursor movement keys are used to select words from the Thesaurus.

    ───

5. There are four ways words can be looked up in WordPerfect's Thesaurus. Name them.

    ───

UNIT

10 MERGING

SUPPLIES NEEDED

1. WordPerfect program disk
2. WordPerfect Student Data disk
3. printer

OBJECTIVES

After completing this unit, you will be able to

1. define the terms "record" and "field";
2. define the terms "primary file" and "secondary file";
3. merge information from primary and secondary files to form one document;
4. use a secondary file to create a new document;
5. merge a primary file with the keyboard;
6. use the Merge Codes menu.

IMPORTANT KEYSTROKES

1. Alt-F9....\....................to display the Merge Codes menu
2. F9..........................to insert a code that identifies the end of a field or to continue a merge after pausing
3. Ctrl-F9....................to start a merge operation
4. Shift-F9...................to insert a code that identifies the end of a record
5. Merge codes:

    ^C...........to stop a merge temporarily so that additional information can be entered from the keyboard
    ^D...........to insert the current date automatically during a merge
    ^E...........to mark the end of a record in a secondary file
    ^O...........to display a message on the status line
    ^Q...........to stop the merge
    ^R...........to mark the end of a field in a secondary file
    ^S...........to link secondary files
    ^P...........to link primary files
    ^T...........to send merged text directly to the printer
    ^N...........to signal the program to look for the next record in the secondary file

ASSIGNMENTS

1. Create a Primary and a Secondary file
2. Merge Files
3. Print Merged Documents
4. Review Questions
5. Research Documentation

MERGING

Merging tasks with a word-processing package means combining data from two or more files to create a new document. Every merging operation requires a **primary file** that contains the text and codes that direct the merge operation. A primary file is merged with variable information from either a secondary file, other user files, or the keyboard.

A **secondary file** is composed of a group of related records (a data base). A **record** is defined as a collection of data items or fields that relate to a single unit. A **field** is defined as a meaningful item of data such as a social security number. The secondary files (your data base) you will generally use for your merge tasks are composed of a group of records (one for each individual) divided into fields of meaningful data (e.g., name, address, age, telephone number)

Merge operations are used primarily by businesses and organizations that frequently mail form letters or organizational notices.   A basic letter is created and stored in the primary file. A record of information on each customer or client is created and stored in the secondary file. Then the two files are merged and a personalized letter is created for each record in the secondary file. It is important to keep the records on the secondary file up to date and complete so that your merging operations are truly efficient.

THE SECONDARY FILE

It is important to create a comprehensive secondary file that contains all the information you need for a merging operation. Each record should contain the same number of fields; each field should have the same type of information. A field can contain any type or length of information. When you have finished entering a field, press F9 (Merge R); the code ^R will be inserted to signify the end of a field.   When you have completed a record, press Shift-F9 (Merge E); the code ^E will be inserted to indicate the end of a record.

GUIDED ACTIVITY: CREATING A SECONDARY FILE

1. Load WordPerfect, taking care to insert the current date.

2. Display a clear screen.

3. Type "Mr. Lawrence Lawson".

4. Press the F9 key.

    You have signified the end of the name field. The ^R will appear on your screen immediately after "Lawson", and the cursor will jump to the next line.

5. Type "46 Emerson Drive".

6. Press the F9 key.

    You have signified the end of the street-address field. The ^R will appear on your screen, and the cursor will jump to the next line.

7. Type "Midland, MO 63724".

8. Press the F9 key to insert the ^R code and signal the end of the city-state-ZIP code field.

9. Type "Lawrence".

10. Press the F9 key.

    You have signified the end of the first-name field and inserted the ^R code.

11. Press the Shift-F9 key.

     You have signified the end of a record and inserted the ^E code. The cursor
     will jump to the next line. Do not insert a <CR> after the ^E.

12. Create another record by repeating the preceding steps; use the following
     information:

     Ms Jane Hanson^R
     26 S. Layton Blvd.^R
     Midland, MO 63724^R
     Jane^R
     ^E

     Both records contain the same number of fields with the same type of
     information.

13. Create another record using the following information:

     Mr. Tom Hogan^R
     16 East River Drive^R
     Midland, MO 63724^R
     Tom^R
     ^E

14. Press F7.

     Save your records under the filename "Namelist.sf". You have created a
     secondary file that will be used for future merge operations.

15. Press <CR> to clear the screen.

✔ CHECKPOINT

     a.   Which key inserts a code at the end of a field?

     _____

     b.   Which key inserts a code at the end of a record?

     _____

What You Have Accomplished

You have created a secondary file, which contains the records of three
individuals. Each record consists of four fields. Each field contains the same
type of information. You have stored your secondary file on your Student Data

disk under the filename **Namelist.sf**. This file will later be merged with another document in a primary file.

Hint: When you are creating your data base (secondary file), never insert a space between the last character in a field and a merge code. Also, be careful to not separate fields with a <CR>.

THE PRIMARY FILE

The primary file usually contains a basic letter with embedded codes to symbolize the placement of variable information from a secondary file. When the Alt-F9 keys are pressed, the Merge Codes menu (Figure 10-1) appears on your screen. From this menu, you may choose a code to insert in your basic letter. You can select a code just by typing the individual letter; the carat (^) is displayed automatically.

^C; ^D; ^F; ^G; ^N; ^O; ^P; ^Q; ^S; ^T; ^U; ^V;

FIGURE 10-1 Merge Codes Menu.

GUIDED ACTIVITY: CREATING A PRIMARY FILE

1. Start with a clear screen. Press Alt-F9.

    The Merge Codes menu will appear on your screen.

2. Type "D".

    "^D" will appear on your screen. You have embedded a code that automatically inserts the current date each time this file is retrieved.

3. Press <CR> three times to create blank lines.

4. Press Alt-F9.

    The Merge Codes menu will appear on your screen.

5. Type "F"

    The prompt "Field Number?:" will appear at the bottom of your screen.

6. Type "1".

7. Press <CR>.

Your screen will look like this: "^F1^". You have embedded a code that will retrieve information from field one (the name field) on your secondary file.

8.   Press <CR>.

9.   Press Alt-F9 to access the Merge Codes menu.

10. Type "F".

The prompt "Field Number?:" will appear at the bottom of your screen.

11. Type "2".

12. Press <CR>.

Your screen will look like this: "^F2^". You have embedded a code that will retrieve information from field two (the street-address field) on your secondary file.

13. Press <CR>.

14. Press Alt-F9 to access the Merge Codes menu.

15. Type "F".

16. Type "3" after the prompt.

17. Press <CR>.

Your screen will look like this: "^F3^". You have embedded a code that will retrieve information from field three (the city-state-ZIP code field) on your secondary file.

18. Press <CR> three times to insert two blank lines between the address and the salutation.

19. Type "Dear".

20. Press <SPACEBAR> once.

21. Press Alt-F9 to display the Merge Codes menu.

22. Type "F", then "4".

23. Press <CR>.

Your screen will look like this: "^F4^". You have embedded a code that will retrieve information from field four (the first-name field).

24. Type ":" (colon).

25. Press <CR> three times to create two blank lines.

26.   Type the following text and codes into the body of your letter (use the default margin settings of 10, 74). Use the Alt-F9 keys to access the Merge Codes menu. The ^C temporarily stops the merge so that you can enter information from the keyboard. The ^O embeds a code that directs the program to display your typed message during a merge operation.

> "This is a reminder that the next meeting of the Long Range Planning Commission will be held on ^O type date of next meeting ^O^C at 7:00 p.m. I have enclosed a copy of the revisions discussed at our last committee meeting.
>
> Please let me know, ^F4^, if there are any items you would like to place on the agenda for the next meeting."

27. Press F7 to Save your file and clear the screen. Name your file "Lrpc.pf".

✔ CHECKPOINT

    c.   Which keys access the Merge Codes menu?

What You Have Accomplished

You have typed a basic form letter that contains all the codes required to merge with the records on a secondary file. You saved this letter in a primary file named **Lrpc.pf**. Now, each time you wish to mail this letter, you can be merge it with your secondary file to create a personalized letter.

MERGING AND PRINTING

When both a primary and a secondary file have been created, merge operations can begin. Each time WordPerfect encounters an ^F, information from a specific field in a record is automatically inserted into your basic letter. Each time WordPerfect encounters a ^C, merge operations are suspended until you insert information from the keyboard and press F9 to continue. Each time WordPerfect encounters an ^E, it directs the printer to end one letter and begin another until all records on the secondary file are used. You may save copies of your completed letters under a new filename.

When you are ready to begin merging, press Ctrl-F9. The Merge/Sort menu (Figure 10-2) will appear. Option 1 on this menu is used for merging.

1 Merge; 2 Sort; 3 Sorting Sequences: 0

FIGURE 10-2, Merge/Sort Menu.

GUIDED ACTIVITY: MERGING AND PRINTING A PERSONALIZED LETTER

1. Press the Ctrl-F9 keys.

    The Merge/Sort menu will appear on the screen.

2. Type "1".

    The prompt "Primary File:" will appear in the status line.

3. Type "Lrpc.pf".

    You have entered the name of your primary file.

4. Press <CR>.

    The prompt "Secondary File:" will appear in the status line.

5. Type "Namelist.sf".

    You have entered the name of your secondary file.

6. Press <CR>.

    Your first merged document has appeared on the screen. Your message "type date of next meeting" is displayed in the status line. The cursor is positioned after the word, "on".

7. Type a date one week from the current date (in response to your message).

8. Press the F9 key to continue the merge operation.

    A hard page break has been inserted and your second merged document has appeared on the screen.

9. Type in the current date; then press F9 to continue merging.

10. Complete the third merged document.

11. Press F7 to Save, and clear your screen. Store your three letters in a file, "Lrpc1.ltr".

✔ CHECKPOINT

d.   Which keys access the Merge/Sort menu?

_____

e.   What happens when the printer encounters an ^O code?

_____

f.   What happens when the printer encounters a ^C code?

_____

What You Have Accomplished

You have merged a primary and a secondary file to create three personalized letters. You stored all three letters in a third file, **Lrpc1.ltr.**

MAILING LABELS

A merge operation can also be used to produce mailing labels. The addresses you need are already stored in your data base in **Namelist.sf.** Another primary file must be created, however, for the mailing labels. Standard paper is used to simulate mailing labels in the following Guided Activity.

GUIDED ACTIVITY: CREATING A PRIMARY FILE FOR MAILING LABELS

1. Make certain you have a clear screen.

2. Press Alt-F9 to access the Merge Codes menu.

3. Type "F".

   The prompt "Field Number?:" will appear in the status line.

4. Type "1".

5. Press <CR> twice.

   Your screen will look like this: "^F1^". You have embedded a code that will retrieve information from field one.

6.   Press Alt-F9 to access the Merge Codes menu.

7.   Type "F", then "2".

8.   Press <CR> twice.

     Your screen will look like this: "^F2^".

9.   Press Alt-F9 to access the Merge Codes menu.

10. Type "F", then "3".

11. Press <CR>.

     Your screen will look like this: "^F3^".

12. Press F7 to Save your newly created file and clear the screen. Name your
     file "Labels.pf".

✔ CHECKPOINT

     g.   Explain what ^F2^ means.

GUIDED ACTIVITY: MERGING FILES TO PRINT MAILING LABELS

1.   Press the Ctrl-F9 keys to access the Merge/Sort menu.

2.   Type "1".

     The prompt "Primary File:" will appear in the status line.

3.   Type "Labels.pf".

     You have identified the name of your primary file.

4.   Press <CR>.

     The prompt "Secondary File:" will appear in the status line.

5.   Type "Namelist.sf".

     You have identified the name of your secondary file.

6.   Press <CR>.

7. Your mailing labels will appear on the screen, each one separated by a hard page break.

8. Press F7 to Save and clear the screen. Name this file, "Labels".

FORMATTING MAILING LABELS

Before merging files to print labels, you must select a label format. Assume that your labels are 1 x 4 inches and single width. (This means that 1-inch labels are arranged one after another on 4-inch-wide continuous-feed paper.)

Setting the Left and Right Margins

At 10 pitch on 4-inch-wide paper, there are forty (4 x 10) horizontal spaces to work with. Set the left margin at 5 and the right margin at 35 to format a page with 1/2-inch-wide margins.

Setting the Top Margin and the Page Length

Vertical lines are determined by measuring from the top of one label to the top of the next. If that measurement is 1 inch, six vertical lines are available for text at the default Print Format setting.   In order to center the three lines of the address on the mailing label, both the top and the bottom margins should be set at one line (or two 1/2-lines).

GUIDED ACTIVITY: PRINTING MAILING LABELS

1. Retrieve the file Labels. Position the cursor at the beginning of the document.

2. Access the Line Format menu to change the margin settings. Set the left margin at 5 and the right margin at 35.

3. Access the Page Length submenu (Option 4 on the Page Format menu) to change the page length. Select option 3 to set the form length to six lines and the number of single-spaced text lines to five.

4. Press <CR>.

5. Select option 5 from the Page Format menu to set the top margin to two 1/2-line spaces.

6. Press <CR> twice.

7.   Press Shift-F7 to display the Print menu.

8.   Type "1" to Print the full text.

9.   Draw a rectangle 1 x 4 inches around each address to see if the formatting was done correctly.

✔ CHECKPOINT

h.   How do you determine the size of a mailing label?

_____

i.   Where do you set the top margin for a 1-inch-wide mailing label?

_____

j.   Which menu is needed to set the right and left margins?

_____

MORE ON MERGING

Merging is a timesaving feature that allows you to print hundreds of form letters while you are using your computer for other purposes. You can merge text from several primary files to assemble one comprehensive document. The code for linking primary files is: ^P(filename)^P. You can also link secondary files to one another. For example, you may create a number of secondary files that fulfill specific mailing requirements; then combine the data from several secondary files for a larger mailing. The code for linking secondary files is ^S(filename)^S.

The automatic printing code (^T) allows you to embed a merge code that sends each merged letter directly to the printer. This code eliminates waiting for the merging operation to be completed before printing the merged letters. A Next code (^N) tells the program to look for the next record in the secondary file and repeat the automatic printing process until all the records in the secondary file have been merged with the primary file. The automatic printing code is efficient except for merge operations that require keyboard entries.

You can stop a merge operation in progress by inserting the Quit command (^Q). Place a ^Q anywhere in either a secondary or primary file and the merging operation will end.

GUIDED ACTIVITY: CREATING A SECONDARY FILE

1. Create a secondary file using the following information: Do not insert a
    <CR> after either of the merge E's (^E).

    Mr. Tom Curran^R
    201 Walnut Dr.^R
    Seattle, WA 32551^R
    Tom^R
    ^E
    Mr. Herb Bergstrom^R
    4319 Norwood Lane^R
    Seattle, WA 34521^R
    Herb^R
    ^E

2. Press Alt-F9.

    The Merge Codes menu will appear on the screen.

3. Type "S".

    An ^S will appear on the screen.

4. Type "B:namelist.sf".

    You have identified the name of the secondary file that you wish to link to
    this secondary file.

5. Press Alt-F9 to access the Merge Codes menu.

6. Type "S".

    An ^S will appear on the screen.

7. Press F7.

    Save these records under the filename "Address1.sf".

8. Press <CR> to clear the screen.

GUIDED ACTIVITY: LINKING SECONDARY FILES

1. Press the Ctrl-F9 keys to acess the Merge/Sort menu.

2. Type "1".

    The prompt "Primary File:" will appear on the screen.

3. Type "Lrpc.pf".

4. Press <CR>.

    The prompt "Secondary File:" will appear on the screen.

5. Type "Address1.sf".

6. Press <CR>.

    Your first merged document will appear on the screen. Make the appropriate keyboard entries when the merge operation stops; then press the F9 key to continue.   After the records in the secondary file **Address1.sf** have been merged with the primary file, the program will merge all the records with the file, "Namelist.sf".

7. Press F7 to Save your merged letters (you now have five merged letters) and Exit the program. Name this file "Lrpc2.ltr".

REVIEW QUESTIONS

1. Explain the meaning of "secondary file" as it is used in merging operations.

    _____

2. Define "record" as it is used to create a data base.

    _____

3. Define "field" as it is used to create a data base.

    _____

4. Which code is used to indicate the end of a field?

    _____

5. Which code is used to indicate the end of a record?

    _____

6. Which code should you choose from the Merge Codes menu to indicate that you have inserted a message in your primary document?

_____

7. If you would like to enter text from your keyboard, which code should you embed in your primary document?

_____

8. Explain the meaning of "primary file" as it is used in merging operations.

_____

9. Explain how to determine the size of a mailing label.

_____

10. What is the most prevalent use for a merge operation?

_____

DOCUMENTATION RESEARCH

1. A secondary file is often referred to as an "address file." How much information can be placed in a secondary file?

_____

2. The fields contained in each record within a secondary file can vary in size. Explain how to enter two address lines in a single field.

_____

3. Suppose that field seven on a secondary file you are creating contains a social security number. Some of your clients, however, do not have social security numbers. How would you handle field seven when creating a record for these individuals?

_____

4. If you are working with a very large secondary file, it is possible that the internal memory capacity of the computer you are using will not be large enough to handle the merge operation. Suggest several ways to solve this problem.

5. Describe how to determine a label format for 1- x 4-inch labels that are arranged in sets of three labels across an 8 1/2- x 11-inch sheet of paper.

UNIT
11 MACROS

SUPPLIES NEEDED

1. WordPerfect program disk
2. WordPerfect Student Data disk
3. printer

OBJECTIVES

After completing this unit, you will be able to

1. create and use macros.

IMPORTANT KEYSTROKES

1. Ctrl-F10.........................to define a macro
2. Alt-F10.........................to start a macro

ASSIGNMENTS

1. Edit **Forfun** Using a Macro
2. Retrieve and Print **Forfun** with a Macro
4. Review Questions
5. Research Documentation

MACROS

When you create a **macro**, you program WordPerfect to do with one keystroke what is normally done with several keystrokes. The macros you create are stored in a file and retrieved whenever they are needed. A macro can consist of commands or commands and text.

A macro is useful for any word-processing task that requires repetitive keystokes. For example, if you type many letters with the same closing, you can store that closing in a macro file; then with a single keystroke you can insert the closing into your document.

A macro can also be used to store a series of commands. For example, you may use the same series of Print Format instructions to prepare your form letters for printing. By placing these instructions in a macro file, you can enter the necessary commands with just one keystroke.

Macros can be chained together, in such a way that several sets (files) of text or commands are executed one after another. A macro can be chained to itself so that the same set (file) of text and commands is repeated a specified number of times.

Your first step in creating a macro is to name it. You can name a permanent macro in two ways: either type a name using two to eight characters or hold down <Alt> while typing a single letter from A to Z.   WordPerfect automatically adds the extension ".mac" to identify the macro file.

To create a temporary macro that will be erased when you Exit WordPerfect, either press <CR> at the end of the macro name or use only a single letter for your macro name.

To start the execution of a macro, press Alt-F10, then type the name of the macro. The text or commands stored in the macro file are automatically inserted into the document you are creating. To start execution of a macro named with the <Alt> key, hold down Alt then type the letter you used to name the macro.

GUIDED ACTIVITY: CREATING A PERMANENT MACRO TO PRINT A DOCUMENT

Turn your printer off while creating this macro.

1. Press the Ctrl-F10 keys.

    The prompt "Define Macro:" will appear in the status line.

2. Type "Print".

You have named this macro file "Print".

3. Press <CR>.

The message "Macro Def" will appear. Each keystroke made from now until the macro has been defined will be stored in this macro file.

4. Press the Shift-F7 keys.

The Print command has been entered into the macro definition. This is the first instruction that will be executed when this macro is retrieved. The Print menu will also appear on the screen.

5. Type "1".

The full-text option (option 1 on the Print menu) has been entered into the macro definition.

6. Press Ctrl-F10 again.

You have completed the task of defining a macro. The "Macro Def" message has disappeared from the status line.

7. Exit and clear the screen.

What You Have Accomplished

You have defined a macro that will print the full text of a document. The macro has been stored in a file named **Print.mac.** Each time you retrieve this file, the full text of the document you are working on will be printed.

✔ CHECKPOINT

a. Which keys are used to define a macro?

b. How is a macro definition ended?

GUIDED ACTIVITY: CREATING A MACRO TO STORE MARGIN SETTINGS

1. Begin with a clear screen.

2. Press the Ctrl-F10 keys to define a macro.

    The prompt "Define Macro:" will appear at the bottom of the screen.

3. Type "Margins".

    You have named a macro file.

4. Press <CR>.

    The message "Macro Def" will appear in the status line. Each keystroke made from now until the macro has been defined will be stored in this macro file.

5. Press the Shift-F8 keys.

    The Line Format menu will appear on the screen.

6. Type "3".

    The prompt "[Margin Set] 10 74 to Left=" will appear in the status line.

7. Type "20".

    The left margin has been reset to 20.

8. Press <SPACEBAR>.

    The prompt "Right =" will appear on your screen.

9. Type "64".

    The right margin has been reset to 64.

10. Press <CR>.

    These margin settings have been stored in the macro file named Margins.mac.

11. Press the Ctrl-F10 keys.

    You have completed the macro definition.

CHECKPOINT

    c. When do you begin defining a macro?

GUIDED ACTIVITY: CREATING A MACRO THAT CONTAINS TEXT

This macro creates a centered heading in a document.   The macro is named with the Alt key.

1.   Begin with a clear screen.

2.   Press the Ctrl-F10 keys to define a macro.

3.   Press the Alt-H keys.

     This macro will be named **Alth.mac**.

4.   Press <CR> four times.

     Four blank lines have been inserted.

5.   Press the <Home>,<Home>,<Up> arrow keys.

6.   Press the Shift-F6 keys to turn on Center.

7.   Type your name.

     Your name will be centered on the first line of a document when this macro is retrieved.

8.   Press <CR> to start a new line.

9.   Press the Shift-F6 keys to activate the Center feature.

10. Type "Unit 11 Macros".

     This title will be centered on the second line of your document when this macro is retrieved.

11. Press <CR> to terminate the Center feature.

12. Press the Ctrl-F10 keys.

     You have completed this macro definition.

✔ CHECKPOINT

     d.   How do you name a macro using the Alt key?

GUIDED ACTIVITY: RETRIEVING A MACRO

Turn your printer on.

1. Clear the screen.

2. Retrieve **Forfun**.

3. Press the Alt-H keys.

    You have retrieved the macro named **Alth.mac**. Two lines of a centered heading will automatically be inserted into your document.

4. Press the Alt-F10 keys.

    The prompt "Macro:" will appear on the screen.

5. Type "Margins".

    You have identified the filename of the macro you wish to retrieve.

6. Press <CR>.

    The margins you specified will be automatically set.

7. Press the Alt-F10 keys to start a macro.

8. Type "Print".

    You have identified the filename of the macro you wish to retrieve.

9. Press <CR>.

    The document **Forfun** will be printed.

10. Press F7 to Exit and Save. Name your document "Forfun2".

✔ CHECKPOINT

e. How do you retrieve a macro?

f. How do you retrieve a macro that was named by using the Alt keys?

What You Have Accomplished

You have retrieved three macros that were stored in separate files on your data storage disk. The text stored in the **Alth.mac** file was automatically inserted into your document. The commands stored in your other two files were automatically executed when the macro was retrieved.

The document **Forfun** was automatically printed with a centered header and adjusted line margins.

Hint: Each macro file you create is listed in the directory. You can identify them by looking for the ".mac" extension. A macro can be retrieved only with the Macro keys. If you attempt to retrieve it with the Retrieve (Shift-F10) or List Files (F5) command, you could damage the macro files.

GUIDED ACTIVITY: CREATING A MACRO CHAIN

This macro will retrieve a file, insert a heading, change the margin settings, and print a document.

1. Begin with a clear screen.

2. Press the Ctrl-F10 keys to define a macro.

    The prompt "Define Macro:" will appear in the status line.

3. Type "Chain" to name this macro.

4. Press <CR>.

    The prompt "Macro Def" will appear in the status line.

5. Press the Shift-F10 keys to Retrieve.

    The prompt "Document to be Retrieved:" will appear in the status line.

6. Type "Forfun".

7. Press <CR>.

    The document, **Forfun**, will appear on the screen.

8. Press the Alt-F10 keys to start the second macro in the chain.

    The prompt "Macro" will appear in the status line.

9. Type "Print" to name the macro you are starting.

10.   Press <CR>.

The prompt "Macro Def" will appear in the status line.

11.   Press the Ctrl-F10 keys.

You have completed the task of defining a macro chain. WordPerfect will save this macro chain under the filename **Chain.mac**.

✔ CHECKPOINT

g.   Which keystrokes are needed to begin the definition of a macro chain?

_____

h.   Which keystrokes are needed to end the defintion of a macro chain?

_____

GUIDED ACTIVITY: USING A MACRO CHAIN

1.   Begin with a clear screen.

2.   Press the Alt-F10 keys.

3.   Type "Chain".

The macro chain **Chain.mac** will be executed.

4.   Exit WordPerfect. Name your file "Forfun3".

What You Have Accomplished

You have created a macro chain that incorporates one of the macros you previously created. When you typed the name of the macro, your document was retrieved and printed.

Hint: Should you change your mind after a macro has started, just press Cancel to stop it.

REVIEW QUESTIONS

1.   What is a macro?

_____

2. What information can be stored in a macro file?

_____

3. What keystrokes are needed to define a macro?

_____

4. How can you stop the execution of a macro once it has begun?

_____

5. Name several word-processing tasks for which macros can be used.

_____

6. What is a macro chain?

_____

7. How do you Retrieve a macro?

_____

DOCUMENTATION RESEARCH

1. It is possible to define a macro with a pause that will let you enter text from the keyboard while the macro is running. Describe how this is done.

_____

2. Which key can be used to repeat a macro a specific number of times?

_____

3. What is a visible macro?

_____

4. There are three basic types of macro chains. Name them.

_____

APPLICATION

SUPPLIES NEEDED

1. WordPerfect program disk
2. WordPerfect Learning disk
3. WordPerfect Student Data disk
4. printer

ASSIGNMENTS

The assignments to be completed for this application section are:

1. Create Lincoln1.txt
2. Create Lincoln2.txt
3. Create Meeting.txt
4. Create Members.lst

GENERAL DIRECTIONS

Application D contains documents you can use to practice the skills you have acquired. You will need to apply both the fundamentals of Part 1 and the special features of Chapters 9, 10 and 11 to reproduce these documents.

The documents offer you the opportunity to practice using the Speller and Thesaurus functions and to create primary and secondary files for merge operations. The document Members.1st gives you a chance to practice macros.

Some instructions have been handwritten on each document. For further guidance, use your template, Quick Reference card, and the WordPerfect user's manual, or refer to the Guided Activities of this workbook.

Retrieve **Lincoln1.txt** from your WordPerfect Student Data disk.   Use   the
WordPerfect Thesaurus disk to return the document to its original form.

Retrieve **Lincoln2.txt** from **your** WordPerfect Student Data disk.   Use   the
WordPerfect Speller disk to correct typographical and spelling errors.

```
Glenn Anderson^R
15976 185th Street^R
Marine, MN 55029^R
Glenn^R
^E
Wilma Lund^R
2301 Lakeaires Blvd.^R
Scandia, MN 55047^R
Wilma^R
^E
George Dahlquist^R
27077 Main Street^R
Forest Lake, MN 55080^R
George^R
^E
Colleen Peterson^R
Rt. 2, Box 808^R
Marine, MN 55032^R
Colleen^R
^E
```

Create a secondary file for a merge operation. Name it Members.sf

Use this file to create and print 1" x 4" mailing labels.

Create a primary file for a merge operation. Name it Meeting.pf

                                        ^D(current date)
                                        flush right

^F1^(name)
^F2^(street address)
^F3^(city, state and zip code)

Dear ^F4^(first name):

We are anxious to have a large turnout at our May parents'
meeting. We have two speakers coming who you may have
heard about.

        Dr. Jeff Turner, who studied gifted students
        in England, France, and Spain, will be joining
        us with tips on how our gifted students can
        profit from exchange programs.

        double indent

        Dr. Janet Freedman, who has been working with
        the gifted at the high school and college
        levels, will also be with us. She will share
        her experiences about the younger high school
        and college students who have been advanced in
        school.

We feel that both speakers have much to offer us. Please
try to attend and enjoy the evening with us.

Post this date on your calendar: Monday, May 3, 1987.

Sincerely,

(your name)

P.S. We are enclosing a copy of the Horizon Newsletter
      and a New Members form.

Enclosures 2

Merge Meeting.pf with Members.sf to create a third document. Name it Meeting.txt

12 pitch
left margin 12
right margin 93

HORIZON CLUB

NEW MEMBERS

Define a macro to create the lines for this list.

NAME   ADDRESS   TELEPHONE

_____   _____   _____

_____   _____   _____

_____   _____   _____

_____   _____   _____

_____   _____   _____

_____   _____   _____

_____   _____   _____

_____   _____   _____

_____   _____   _____

_____   _____   _____

_____   _____   _____

_____   _____   _____

_____   _____   _____

_____   _____   _____

_____   _____   _____

_____   _____   _____

Name this document Members.lst   _____

UNIT

12 COLUMNS

SUPPLIES NEEDED

1. WordPerfect program disk
2. WordPerfect Student Data disk
3. printer

OBJECTIVES

After completing this unit, you will be able to

1. define a newspaper column;
2. define a parallel column.

IMPORTANT KEYSTROKES

1. Alt-F7..........................to create text columns

ASSIGNMENTS

1.   Create Wordperf.col
2.   Create Parallel.col
3.   Review Questions
4.   Research Documentation

TEXT COLUMNS

Text columns are distinguished from **numeric** columns because they are set up to make it convenient to enter text. Text is entered into one column to the end of the page or until you command the column function to terminate. The following text is then entered into the next defined column, and so on, until the page is filled. In text columns you cannot tab from column to column as you do in numeric columns.

Both parallel columns and newspaper columns can be created with WordPerfect. In newspaper columns, text flows from the bottom of one column to the top of the next column. In parallel columns, related groups of text are placed side by side (as, for example, in comparison tables).

Two to five text columns can be defined. Defining columns is much like setting margins, except that the task is done automatically. The column format you have defined appears on your screen as well as on the printed document.

THE MATH/COLUMNS MENU

When you press Alt-F7, the Math/Columns menu (Figure 12-1) appears on your screen. The first two options on this menu are used to set up numeric columns for mathematical calculations. The last three options are used to define, start, and display text columns. Select an option by typing one of the listed numbers.

1 Math On; 2 Math Def; 3 Column On/Off; 4 Column Def; 5 Column Display: 0

FIGURE 12-1 Math/Columns Menu.

The Column feature options are defined as follows (Options 1 and 2 apply to math columns and are discussed in Unit 14):

3   Column On/Off. This option is selected when you wish to either begin or end the Column feature. When the Column feature is turned on, a [Col On] code is placed in your document and a "Col" message appears in the status line. When the Column feature is turned off, a [Col Off] code is placed in your text and the "Col" message disappears from your

status line. Columns must first be defined before the Column feature can be turned on.

4 Column Def. The Text Column Definition submenu (Figure 12-2) appears. With this submenu, you can define the style, width, and number of text columns you wish to create.

```
Text Column Definition

   Do you wish to have evenly spaced columns?(Y/N)
   If yes, number of spaces between columns:
   Do you want groups kept together on a page?(Y/N) N
   Number of text columns (2-5)0

   Column margins      Left      Right
     Column 1:
     Column 2:
     Column 3:
     Column 4:
     Column 5:
```

FIGURE 12-2   Text Column Definition Submenu.

Guidelines for defining text columns:

If you want your columns to be the same width, WordPerfect will automatically calculate the margin settings and display them on this submenu. You must designate the number of text columns (2-5) and the number of spaces between columns.

If you would like columns of varying widths, type "N" after the prompt "Do you wish to have evenly spaced columns?(Y/N)".

If you wish to set up parallel columns, type "Y" after the prompt "Do you want groups kept together on a page?(Y/N) N". A block protection code will be inserted to keep groups of text together.

5 Column display. The prompt "Display columns side by side?(Y/N) Y" is displayed.

GUIDED ACTIVITY: CREATING A NEWSPAPER COLUMN

1. Retrieve Wordperf.

2. Move the cursor to the beginning of the document.

3. Press the Alt-F7 keys.

    The Math/Columns menu will appear on the screen.

4. Type "4".

    The Text Column Definition submenu will appear.

5. Type "Y" after the prompt "Do you wish to have evenly spaced columns?(Y/N)".

6. Type "5" after the prompt "If yes, number of spaces between columns:".

7. Press <CR>.

8. Type "N" (or press <CR> to accept the default setting, N) after the prompt "Do you want groups kept together on a page? (Y/N) N".

    You have selected newspaper-style columns, which does not require that related groups of information be kept together.

9. Press <CR>.

10. Type "2" after the prompt "Number of text columns (2-5)0".

    The margins for the two columns will be automatically calculated and then displayed in the Column Margin table on the Text Column Definition submenu.

11. Press <CR> several times to return to the Math/Columns menu screen.

12. Type "3" to turn on the Columns feature.

13. Move the cursor to the end of the document. The columns form automatically on the screen. The left column fills to the end of the page before text is entered into the right column.

14. Move the cursor to the blank line above the heading "The top seller.".

15. Press the Ctrl-<CR> keys to create a Hard Page break. The remainder of the left column will be moved to the top of the right column.

16. Press <CR> to align the topic headers in columns 1 and 2.

17. Move the cursor to the bottom of the right column.

18. Press the Alt-F7 keys.

    The Math/Columns menu will appear on the screen.

19. Type "3" to turn off the Columns feature.

20. Name this document "Wordperf.col".

21. Save and Print **Wordperf.col**.

✔ CHECKPOINT

a. How do you use the Text Column Definition submenu to create newspaper columns?

_____

b. How do you turn on the Columns feature?

_____

What You Have Accomplished

You have reformatted the text of **Wordperf.txt** to be printed in two newspaper columns. The margins for these columns were automatically calculated. You inserted a [Col On] code to begin the Column feature and a [Col Off] code to end it.

GUIDED ACTIVITY: CREATING PARALLEL COLUMNS

1. Display a clear screen.

2. Press the Alt-F7 keys to display the Math/Columns menu.

3. Type "4".

    The Text Column Definition submenu will appear.

4. Type "Y" to select evenly-spaced columns.

5. Type "3".

    You have chosen to place three spaces between each of your columns.

6. Press <CR>.

7. Type "Y" to select parallel-style columns.

    Groups of related information will be kept together on a page.

8. Type "3".

    You have chosen to create three columns. The margins of each column will be calculated automatically and displayed on the Text Column Definition submenu.

9. Press <CR> until the Math/Columns menu reappears on the screen.

10. Type "3" to turn on the Column feature.

11. Type "Lawrence Lawson".

12. Press the Ctrl-<CR> keys to wrap to the second column.

13. Type the following address in column 2:

        46 Emerson Drive
        Midland, MO 63724

14. Press the Ctrl-<CR> keys to wrap to the third column.

15. Type the following telephone number in column 3:

        612-456-9146

16. Press the Ctrl-<CR> keys to wrap to the beginning of the first column.

17. Repeat steps 11 through 16 to enter the following records in parallel columns:

        Jane Hanson
        26 S. Layton Blvd.
        Midland, MO 63724
        622-789-5555

        Tom Hogan
        16 East River Drive
        Midland, MO 63724
        632-457-9263

18. Press the Alt-F7 keys.

    The Math/Columns menu will appear on the screen.

19. Type "3" to turn off the Column feature.

20. Name this file "Parallel.col".

21. Save and Print **Parallel.col.**

Hint: Each of the columns you have defined is independent of all the others. You can move the cursor independently in one column to add or delete text without affecting the text in the neighboring columns.

✔ CHECKPOINT

    c.   Which keys are used to wrap to the next column?

_____

    d.   How do you define parallel columns?

_____

What You Have Accomplished

You have learned that parallel columns are defined in a slightly different manner than are newspaper columns. Block protection codes are placed around related groups of information to protect them from a page break.

REVIEW QUESTIONS

1.   Explain the difference between a newspaper column and a parallel column.

_____

2.   Which option on the Math/Columns submenu would you choose to turn on the Column feature.

_____

3.   Suppose that you have decided to use WordPerfect to produce your company newsletter. In what order would you perform the following tasks? (a) type the articles that will be contained in the newsletter; (b) turn on the Columns feature; (c) establish the width of your columns.

_____

4.   Which text column style would you choose to display related information side by side? Describe how to select this style.

_____

5.   Describe how an existing document is reformatted into text columns.

_____

DOCUMENTATION RESEARCH

1. How is text centered over a column?

    _____

2. How are parallel columns protected from page breaks that could separate
    related groups of text?

    _____

3. Describe how the cursor movement keys are used to edit text columns.

    _____

UNIT

13 TABLE OF CONTENTS, LISTS, AND INDEXES

SUPPLIES NEEDED

1. WordPerfect program disk
2. WordPerfect Student Data disk
3. printer

OBJECTIVES

After completing this unit, you will be able to

1. mark text to create a table of contents.

IMPORTANT KEYSTROKES

1. Alt-F5.........................to mark text for a list, a table of contents, or an index.

ASSIGNMENTS

1.   Create a Table of Contents
2.   Review Questions
3.   Research Documentation

TABLES OF CONTENTS, LISTS, and INDEXES

One of WordPerfect's special features is its capability to generate a table of contents, a list of figures or illustrations, or an index. This is especially useful for very long documents.

A table of contents, list, or index is created by using text from your document. Codes, [Mark] and [End Mark], must be inserted into the document to mark the text you will use. You can generate a table of contents with up to five levels of heads, or as many as five different lists, or an index with both headings and subheadings.

The table of contents, list, or index you generate will most likely require page references. WordPerfect offers five different styles for numbering pages. A code must be placed in the text to define a numbering style.

MARKING TEXT

To mark text, turn Block on, move the cursor movement keys across the text you want in your contents, list or index, then press Alt-F5 (the Mark Text keys). The Mark Text menu (Figure 13-1) will appear on your screen. Select the option that identifies the feature you are creating by typing one of the listed numbers (1, 2, or 5).

Options 3 and 4 are identical to options 3 and 4 on the Mark Text menu (with Block off) and are defined on the following page.

```
1 Table of Contents; 2 List; 3 Redline; 4 Strikeout; 5 Index: 0
```

FIGURE 13-1 Mark Text Menu (Block On).

When you press the Alt-F5 keys with Block off, the Mark Text menu (Figure 13-2) contains different options. This menu is used to mark a single index word, to define a numbering style, and to generate your contents, list, or index.

1 Outline; 2 Para #; 3 Redline; 4 Remove; 5 Index; 6 Define; 7 Generate: 0

FIGURE 13-2   Mark Text Menu (Block Off).

The Mark Text menu options (with Block off) are defined as follows:

1 Outline.   When you select this option, a [Para #] code is inserted into your document.   That code instructs the program to insert paragraph numbers to create an outline.   Each time you edit your outline, it will be automatically renumbered.

2 Para #.   A paragraph numbering code is placed in your document and the correct numbering level appears on the screen.   Paragraph numbers can be automatic or fixed.

3 Redline.   This option is used to mark text for possible revision.   It is useful when you are editing someone else's document.   Text that has been redlined will be printed with a vertical bar in the left margin.

4 Remove.   This option removes redline markings.

5 Index.   The prompt "Index Heading" appears.   The word at the cursor location appears beside the prompt.   If you prefer to enter your own heading, type over the one displayed.   Then press <CR> and the prompt "Subheading" appears.   Type a subheading if you want one.   If you entered your own heading after the first prompt, the word at the cursor location appears again.   Press <CR> to use the displayed text for a subheading or <BACKSPACE> and type your own subheading.

6 Define. The Text Marking Definition submenu (Figure 13-3) appears on the screen.   With this option, you can define a numbering style for the list, table of contents, or index you are creating.

The options on this submenu are used to select the feature (contents, list, or index) you wish to create.   With each option selection, a submenu that offers five different numbering styles is displayed.   The Table of Contents Definition submenu (Figure 13-4) offers five levels that can each be numbered in a unique style.

```
Text Marking Definition

    1 - List 1
    2 - List 2
    3 - List 3
    4 - List 4
    5 - List 5
    6 - Table of Contents
    7 - Paragraph/Outline Numbering
    8 - Index

Selection: 0
```

FIGURE 13-3   Text Marking Definition Submenu.

```
Table of Contents Definition

    Number of levels in table of contents (1-5): 0

                    Page Number Position
    Level 1
    Level 2
    Level 3
    Level 4
    Level 5

    Page Number Position
    1 - No Page Numbers
    2 - Page Number Follow Entries
    3 - (Page Numbers) follow Entries
    4 - Flush Right Page Numbers
    5 - Flush Right Page Numbers with Leaders
```

FIGURE 13-4   Table of Contents Definition Submenu.

7 Generate. When you select this option, the list, table of contents, or index you have defined is created. This prompt appears: "Have you deleted your old Table of Contents, Lists, and Index? (Y/N) N". A counter at the bottom of your computer screen keeps you informed of the program's progress.

GUIDED ACTIVITY: CREATING A TABLE OF CONTENTS

1. Retrieve Educate.txt.

2. Block the title of the document.

3. Press the Alt-F5 keys.

    The Mark Text menu will appear.

4. Type "1".

    The prompt "ToC Level:" will appear in the status line.

5. Type "1" to indicate a first-level heading.

6. Block the topic heading "Forces of Change".

7. Press the Alt-F5 keys to display the Mark Text menu.

8. Type "1" to select Table of Contents.

    The prompt "ToC Level:" will appear in the status line.

9. Type "2" to indicate a second-level heading.

10. Scroll through the document until you find another topic heading. Repeat
    steps 6 through 9 until all second-level headings have been marked.

11. Move the cursor a few lines below the text of Educate.txt.

12. Press the Ctrl-<CR> keys to create a Hard Page break.

13. Type "TABLE OF CONTENTS".

14. Press the <CR> twice to insert a blank line.

15. Press the Alt-F5 keys to display the Mark Text menu.

16. Type "6" to display the Text Marking Definition submenu.

17. Type "6" to display the Table of Contents Definition submenu.

    The prompt "Number of levels in table of contents (1-5): 0" will appear.

18. Type "2".

    You have indicated that there are two levels of entries in your table of
    contents.

The prompt "Display last level in wrapped format? (Y/N) N" will appear.

19. Type "N".

The last level (second-level) will not be displayed in wrapped format.

20. The default page number position "(5)" will appear on the screen.

21. Press <CR> twice to accept the default and return to your document.

22. Press the Alt-F5 keys again to display the Mark Text menu.

23. Type "7".

The prompt "Have you deleted your old Table of Contents, Lists and Index? (Y/N) N" will appear on the screen.

24. Type "Y" to indicate that there is no other table of contents, list or index defined.

The prompt "Generation in progress. Counter:" will appear in the status line while the table is being generated.

In a few seconds the table of contents for Educate.txt will appear on the screen.

25. Save Educate.txt.

26. Print the table of contents page.

✔ CHECKPOINT

a. Which keys are needed to access the Mark Text menu?

_____

b. What is the first step in marking text for a table of contents?

_____

c. Which option is needed to generate a table of contents?

_____

What You Have Accomplished

You have used the Block key and the Mark Text menu to create a table of contents. Your table of contents contains two levels of heads. Each header of your table also contains a page reference, which will be printed Flush Right on the same line as the header.

REVIEW QUESTIONS

1. How many headings are available for generating a table of contents?

2. How many lists can be generated from a single document?

3. Explain the procedure you would use to enter a subheading into an index.

4. List the five different numbering styles you can use to create an index, list, or table of contents.

DOCUMENTATION RESEARCH

1. What is the difference between redline and strikeout? How does the marking of text differ in these two features?

2. How does one select a legal numbering style for an outline?

3. The Mark text menu contains different options that depend on whether Block is on or off. Both menus, however, contain option 5, Index. Explain the difference between these two options.

UNIT

14 MATH

SUPPLIES NEEDED

1. WordPerfect program disk
2. WordPerfect Student Data disk
3. printer

OBJECTIVES

After completing this unit, you will be able to

1. calculate subtotals, totals, and grand totals in a vertical column;
2. define numeric and calculation columns.

IMPORTANT KEYSTOKES

1. Alt-F7.............................to use the Math feature

ASSIGNMENTS

1. Create a Math Document

THE MATH FEATURE

With WordPerfect's Math feature, you can add, subtract, multiply, and divide up to twenty-four columns of numbers. When you create a math document , you need both text columns and numeric columns. Text columns are used for descriptions and labels. Numeric columns contain numbers that are used in calculations.

The first step in establishing numeric columns is to set tabs. Keep in mind that the columns must be wide enough to contain all the digits of your longest number. Most calculations are done in vertical columns, but columns can also be set so that calculations are performed across columns.

The process of setting up columns for math calculations is tedious, but once the columns are set up, they can be used for both macros and merges. Although WordPerfect's Math feature is sophisticated, it cannnot substitute for a spreadsheet. Therefore, carefully consider the applications for this feature before going through the effort of setting it up.

THE MATH DEFINITION MENU

When the Math/Columns key (Alt-F7) is pressed, the Math/Columns menu (Figure 14-1) appears. Select an option by typing one of the listed numbers.

1 Math On; 2 Math Def; 3 Column On/Off; 4 Column Def; 5 Column Display: 0

FIGURE 14-1 Math/Columns Menu.

The Math options on this menu are defined as follows:

1 Math On. A [Math On] code is placed in your document. A "Math" message appears in the status line. This message must always be present when you wish to create, edit, or calculate a math document. Columns must first be defined before Math is turned on.

2 Math Def. The Math Definition (Figure 14-2) submenu appears on your screen. With this submenu, you can define numeric and text columns.

Math Definition   Use arrow keys to position cursor

Columns   A B C D E F G H I J K L M N O P Q R S T U V W X

Type   2 2 2 2 2 2 2 2 2 2 2 2 2 2 2 2 2 2 2 2 2 2 2 2

Negative Numbers   (

# of digits to   2 2 2 2 2 2 2 2 2 2 2 2 2 2 2 2 2 2 2 2 2 2 2 2
the right (0-4)

Calculation   1
Formulas   2
              3
              4

Type of Column:
    0 = Calculation   1 = Text   2 = Numeric   3 = Total

Negative Numbers
    (= Parenthesis (50.00)   - = Minus Sign -50.00

Press EXIT when done

FIGURE 14-2 Math Definition Submenu.

Guidelines for Defining Columns:

You can set up to twenty-four numeric columns, but only four can be
designated as calculation columns. It is important to make the columns
wide enough to contain your longest number. If the columns overlap, the
calculations will not be correct.

Four types of columns can be defined.   Numeric columns are used for
constants, totals, subtotals, and grand totals. Text columns are used
for descriptions and labels. Total columns are used for displaying
totals from all the columns to the left. Calculation columns contain
equations to calculate data across columns. The default setting is
numeric which means that unless you designate otherwise, all columns
are treated as numeric columns except for the first column, which is
reserved for labeling your math document.

Negative numbers may be displayed either in parentheses or with a minus
sign. The default is set for parentheses.

There may be from zero to four digits to the right of a decimal point. The default setting is two.

Options 3, 4, and 5 on the Math Definition submenu are used to set up newspaper columns or parallel columns.

GUIDED ACTIVITY: SETTING TABS

The first step in preparing a math document is to set the tab stops. These tab stops determine the width of each column you will later define.

1.   Begin with a clear screen.

2.   Access the Line Format menu (Shift-F8) to change the tab stops. Set the tab stops at 40, 60, and 80.

GUIDED ACTIVITY: DEFINING COLUMNS

1.   Press the Alt-F7 keys.

     The Math/Columns menu will appear on your screen.

2.   Type "2".

     The Math Definition submenu will appear.

3.   Move the cursor to the Type row in the A column.

4.   Type "2".

     You have defined a numeric column. Notice the definitions under the header Type of Column on this submenu.

5.   Move the cursor to "# of digits to the right (0-4)" in the A column.

6.   Type "0".

     You have indicated that there will be no digits to the right of the decimal point in column A.

7.   Move the cursor to the Type row in the B column.

8.   Type "0".

     You have defined a calculation column. The cursor will move automatically to Calculation Formulas on this submenu and a "B" will appear after the "1".

9. Type "A*1.1".

You have specified the mathematical formula to be used in the calculation column, column B. All of the numbers in column A will be multiplied by 1.1 (110%).

10. Press <CR> to enter the formula.

11. Press F7 to Exit the Math Definition submenu.

12. Type "0" or press <CR> to clear the screen.

✔ CHECKPOINT

a.   Which keys are used to access the Math/Columns menu?

_____

b.   Explain how to define a numeric column on the Math Definition submenu.

_____

c.   How does the cursor respond when a calculation column is selected?

_____

d.   Which key do you press when you have completed the task of defining columns?.

_____

What You Have Accomplished

You have used the Math Definition submenu to define two columns, a numeric column and a calculation column. You have also determined the width of these columns by changing the tab stop settings. Column A (the numeric column) begins at the first tab stop; column B (the calculation column) begins at the second tab stop. The first column (the space between the left margin and the first tab stop) is reserved for labeling your math document.

GUIDED ACTIVITY: CREATING A BUDGET WORKSHEET

This Guided Activity for creating a Math document is a lengthy one. Refer to Figure 14-3 to enter the values and labels required.

1. With the cursor at Ln 1 of the clear screen, type "ABC Corporation".

2. Press <CR>.

3. Type "Budget Report for 1987".

    You have entered a title for your budget worksheet.

4. Press <CR> twice.

5. Type "Budget Items".

    You have labeled the first column (the labels column).

6. Press <SPACEBAR> thirteen times.

7. Type "Total".

    You have labeled column A.

8. Press <SPACEBAR> fifteen times.

9. Type "Next Year 110%".

    You have labeled column B.

10. Press <CR> twice.

11. Press the Alt-F7 key.

    The Math/Columns menu will reappear on the screen.

12. Type "1".

    You have turned the Math feature on. The message "Math" will appear in the status line.

13. Type "Advertising".

    You have identified your first budget item and labeled the first row.

14. Press <TAB>.

15. Type "2,000".

    You have identified the value of your first budget item, which has been placed in column A (the numeric column).

16. Press <TAB>.

    An ! has been automatically inserted into column B because you defined it as a calculation column.

✔ CHECKPOINT

e.   Which column in your math document is reserved for labels?

_____

f.   How is the Math feature turned on?

_____

g.   How does the WordPerfect program signal that a column has been defined as a calculation column?

_____

17. Press <CR> once.

18. Type "Travel".

You have identified the second budget item and labeled the second row.

19. Press <TAB>.

20. Type "800".

You have identified the second value to be placed in column A.

21. Press <TAB>.

An ! will appear in column B.

22. Press <CR> twice.

23. Press <SPACEBAR> twice.

24. Type "Subtotal".

25. Press <TAB>.

26. Type "+".

You have inserted an operator. The numbers above the operator in column A will be added and displayed in the row labeled Subtotal.

27. Press <TAB>.

28. Press <CR> twice.

29. Refer to Figure 14-3. Enter the next two budget item labels and their corresponding values. Also enter "Subtotal" and the operator "+".

30.   Press <CR> twice.

The cursor should be in the first column.

31.   Type "Total".

32.   Press <TAB>.

33.   Type "=".

You have inserted an operator. The subtotals (the results of the "+" operator) above this operator in column A will be added and displayed in the row labeled Total.

34.   Press <TAB>.

An ! will appear in column B.

35.   Press <CR> twice.

✔ **CHECKPOINT**

h.   What happens when the operator "=" is inserted into your math document?

Hint: WordPerfect does not perform calculations in text columns. Therefore you may use numbers as labels in the first column. Keep in mind that the Math feature (option 1 on the Math/Columns menu) must be turned on before you can create or edit a math document. As long as the "Math" message is displayed at the bottom of your screen, your math calculations will take place as they should.

GUIDED ACTIVITY: CALCULATING THE BUDGET WORKSHEET

1.   Press the Alt-F7 keys.

The Math/Columns menu will appear on your screen. With the "Math" message on the screen, option 2 is "Calculate" instead of "Math Def".

2.   Type "2".

The calculations will take place and the results displayed in column B. Your printed document will look like that in Figure 14-4. The document on your screen displays the symbols representing the math operations. The budget report will not, however, contain those symbols when it is printed.

What You Have Accomplished

You have created a Math document (a budget report). Your document contains both text columns for labels and numeric columns for numbers and mathematical formulas.

You calculated the numbers in the numeric columns by inserting operators. Then you chose an option from the Math/Columns menu that automatically performed calculations using the formula you placed in column B when you defined your columns. You now have a completed budget report.

```
ABC Corporation
Budget Report for 1987

Budget Items              Total              Next Year 110%

Advertising               2,000                    !
Travel                      800                    !

  Subtotal                   +                     !

Printing                    500                    !
Education                   700                    !

  Subtotal                   +                     !

Total                        =                     !
```

FIGURE 14-3   Uncalculated Budget Report.


```
ABC Corporation
Budget Report for 1987

Budget Items              Total              Next Year 110%

Advertising               2,000              2,200.00
Travel                      800                880.00

  Subtotal               2,800              3,080.00

Printing                    500                550.00
Education                   700                770.00

  Subtotal               1,200              1,320.00

Total                     4,000              4,400.00
```

FIGURE 14-4   Calculated and Printed Budget Report.

GUIDED ACTIVITY: TURNING OFF THE MATH FEATURE

1. Press the Alt-F7 keys.

2. Type "1".

    The Math feature has been turned off and the "Math" message has disappeared from your screen. You can insert additional text if you like, but any time you wish to make changes to the budget report, Math must be turned on again.

3. Save and Print the budget report. Name this file Budget.rpt.

✔ CHECKPOINT

i.   What menu option must you choose to automatically insert results into a calculation column?

_____

j.   What two steps are needed to turn off the Math feature?

_____

REVIEW QUESTIONS

1. What is the main purpose of WordPerfect's Math feature?

_____

2. Explain how the Math feature is turned on?

_____

3. Describe the contents of each of the four types of columns that can be defined.

    a. _____

    b. _____

    c. _____

    d. _____

4. What is a calculation column? How many can be set up?

_____

5. What is a numeric column? How many can be set up?

    ===

6. What is the major difference between text columns and numeric columns?

    ===

7. Describe how an operator functions.

    ===

8. How do you turn off the Math feature?

    ===

9. How do you set column widths?

    ===

DOCUMENTATION RESEARCH

1. What are the two ways to display negative values in a math document?

    ===

2. What operator is needed to calculate a grand total?

    ===

3. How can you insert extra totals and subtotals?

    ===

4. Which four operators are used to create a mathematical formula?

    ===

5. When there are two or more operators, they are calculated from left to right. How can you change the order of calculation?

    ===

APPLICATION

SUPPLIES NEEDED

1. WordPerfect program disk
2. WordPerfect Learning disk
3. WordPerfect Student Data disk
4. printer

ASSIGNMENTS

The assignments to be completed for this application section are:

1. Create **Minutes.txt**
2. Create **Clinic.txt**
3. Create **Newsltr.txt**

GENERAL DIRECTIONS

Application E contains documents you can use to practice the skills you have acquired. You will need to apply both the fundamentals of Part 1 and the special features of Part 2 to reproduce these documents.

The documents offer you the opportunity to practice writing reports, creating parallel columns, writing newsletters and creating primary and secondary files for merge operations. The document **Members.1st** gives you a chance to practice macros.

Some instructions have been handwritten on each document. For further guidance, use your template, Quick Reference card, and the WordPerfect user's manual, or refer to the Guided Activities of this workbook.

LAKEWOOD SCHOOL
LAND DEVELOPMENT COMMITTEE

Name this document Minutes.txt

MINUTES
MARCH 22, 1987

Center heading

10 pitch
left margin 10
right margin 74

Present: Don Lord, Jeff Albert, Glenn Maki, John Nelson, Bob
White, Les Carlson, Tom Bryant, John Richards

We discussed covering the nature path with wood chips. We may
have to use a chemical spray to kill weeds. We will check into
the Wild Life Packet (7 or 8 bushes) that is supposed to attract
and keep birds.

Plantings (seedlings)

Norway Pine	500	$215.00	
White Spruce	500	230.80	*use*
Scotch Pine	500	210.00	*tab*
Green Ash	100	68.35	*align*
Norway Spruce	500	240.00	
Black Walnut	100	112.75	
Total			

Dates: Saturday, April 20th . . . . . Clearing and chipping
          Saturday, April 27th . . . . . Planting of trees

Bring: Chain saws, planting bars, wheelbarrows, shovels,
rakes, sprayers

Center   PUT THESE DATES ON YOUR SCHEDULE!

Assignments:

    Les Carlson -- pick up trees at Willow Creek or at some
    other location specified by the grower

    Don Lord ----- obtain larger plantings

    Jeff Albert -- get the chemical spray to kill weeds

    Les Carlson -- order the trees

We need at least twenty people on each of the above dates.

(Center heading)

CEDAR HILLS MEDICAL CLINIC
2631 CEDAR LANE
MORRIS, MICHIGAN 56031
621/456-3189

10 pitch
left margin 10
right margin 74

September 3, 1986
flush right

The following physicians have recently joined our full-time medical staff:

Theresa F. Schmitt, M.D.

Create 2 parallel columns with 5 spaces between columns.

Pediatrician. Earned her medical degree at Stanford University in 1971. Interned at Ramsey County General Hospital. Board-certified by the American Board of Pediatrics.

John M. Clark, M.D.

Obstetrician and Gynecologist. Received his medical degree from the University of Minnesota in 1978. Junior Fellow of the American College of Obstetrics and Gynecology.

Brian T. Tuma, M.D.

Internist. Earned his medical degree at Duke University. Completed advanced training in California. Board-certified by the American Board of Internal Medicine.

Name this document Clinic.txt

12 pitch
Margins 12, 93

HORIZON NEWSLETTER

SHARE YOUR IDEAS   *3 spaces between columns!*

Parents, do you have some special things you do with your children, or do you know of some "neat" places to visit as a family that you can share with us? We would like to publish some ideas in the coming issues -- things to do with children. If you can share ideas with us, please send them to Horizon Newsletter at the Lakewood School. We appreciate your help and support.

ADVISORY COUNCIL NOTES

February 22nd meeting: A brief meeting was held at Lakewood School. The field trip to the Children's Theatre was cancelled because not enough people had signed up to go. March 11th is the date for the next general meeting, on the topic of creativity. Possible dates considered for the next meeting are the first or second week in May. Suggestions from the parents for topics are welcome. Other discussion centered around the need for more parental input for the newsletter and the need for parental awareness of changes taking place in the district.

March 10th meeting: Mr. Johnson reported that programs for the gifted on the elementary and middle school levels are going well. He hopes to have a formal program for the high school on paper and in operation by next fall.

Articles and drawings are coming in slowly for the literary magazine "Beyond the Horizon." If not enough material is submitted, publication will probably be through the monthly newsletter.

The next field trip will be scheduled for the last week in April. It will be a low-cost expedition.

HORIZON CHESS INVITATIONAL

The Horizon Program will sponsor an invitational tournament on Saturday, March 20th, at the Lakewood School. The tournament will be divided into three sections:
1. Unrated Juniors (under 18)
2. Rated Juniors
3. Unrated Adults (over 18)

We will play 40 moves an hour and individuals are encouraged to bring their own boards and clocks with them. Rated players will be required to record their moves. Parents who would like to participate in any way with this tournament should call Steve Johnson at 225-6300. Parent involvement will be greatly appreciated.

WERE YOU THERE

The topic at the March parents' meeting at the Lakewood School concerned creativity and creative problem-solving. The parents viewed an interesting film about creative problem-solving and then discussed creativity, especially in the field of musical giftedness. The speaker for the evening was Virginia Curry. After an interesting question-and-answer session about musical giftedness, the parents adjourned to small discussion groups for the remainder of the evening. A special thank-you to all the parents in attendance, and to Virginia Curry for sharing her experiences with us.

If you have any ideas for a May meeting, please contact Steve Johnson at 225-6300. All ideas are welcome and appreciated.

A GETTING STARTED ON YOUR MICROCOMPUTER

Laura B. Ruff
Mary K. Weitzer
Steve C. Ross

This appendix covers the knowledge necessary to use application software with the IBM PC or compatible microcomputers along with the disk operating system (DOS). It is not intended to make you an expert in DOS, but rather to provide some level of competence by providing the necessary operations external to the software discussed in this manual.

PART I: THE KEYBOARD

The IBM and other personal computers have over eighty keys, about forty more than most typewriters. An illustration of the keyboard appears inside the back cover. Many of the "extra" keys have symbols or mnemonics rather than characters. This illustration includes the WordPerfect template which identifies the purpose of each function key. To minimize confusion, the following conventions are used in Understanding and Using WordPerfect.

Conventions

Several typographical conventions have been established to improve readability and understanding. They were established to clearly communicate each WordPerfect function. They are as follows:

When a keystroke activates a single command, it is designated like this: <KEYNAME> (e.g., <CR>, <SPACEBAR>).

The keys that direct cursor movement are designated, for example, like these: <Up>, <Down>, <Left>, <Right>, <Home>, <End>, <PgUp>.

When one key is used in combination with another, the first one must be held down while the other is pressed. Combination keys are separated by a hyphen (e.g., Alt-F4).

When keys are pressed one after another but not in combination, they are separated by a comma (e.g., <Home>,<Home>,<Right> arrow).

All functions begin with a capital letter (e.g., Exit, Save, Cancel).

FUNCTION KEYS

These ten keys are located in two columns along the left edge of the keyboard. Most application software packages make special use of these keys. Although these keys also have special meanings when used by DOS, we ignore those uses here to avoid confusion with the application program that is the subject of this book.

MULTIPLE KEY COMBINATIONS

On a typewriter, the Shift is used in conjunction with a letter key to produce a capital letter. The same is true on a computer. On a computer, the Ctrl and Alt keys act as modifying keys; if either of these keys is used in conjunction with another key, the original letter is modified. These keys are manipulated in the same manner as the Shift key; for example, to type "Alt-M", hold down the Alt key and type "M".

WHAT IS A "TOGGLE" KEY

Toggle keys act as on-off switches. Press them once and they are activated; press them a second time and they are deactivated. Examples of toggle keys include the <NUM LOCK> key (activates the numeric keypad), the Ctrl-<PrtSc> combination (prints the current screen when in DOS), and the <CAPS LOCK> key.

CAPS LOCK KEY

The <CAPS LOCK> key shifts all alphabet (A...Z) keys to upper-case but has no affect on any key that does not contain a letter. (in this it is unlike the shift lock key of a typewriter, which locks all keys into shifted characters).   The <CAPS LOCK> key is a toggle key.

NUMERIC KEYPAD KEYS

The numeric keypad keys, on the right side of the keyboard, are configured as a ten-key pad. The keys with arrows on them are referred to as arrow keys or as <Up>, <Left>, <Down>, and <Right>. The other keypad keys are referred to by the text that appears on them: <Home>, <PgUp>, <PgDn>, <End>, <DEL>, and <INS>. The numeric function of the keys can be activated by using the <Num Lock> key (a toggle key). Most of these keys have no affect in DOS, but they are used by many application programs to control movement on the screen.

PART II: GETTING STARTED

LOADING DOS

Loading DOS means that some of the DOS programs are read from the DOS disk to load the system before loading the application program. Other application software gives you instructions on how to install DOS onto the software program disk in order to make it self-loading and how to attain some system capabilities without switching disks.

DOS PROMPT

The DOS or system prompt ("A>" with a single or dual drive system or "C>" with a hard disk) tells you that it is your turn to type information; that is, you must tell DOS what to do by entering a command.

The system prompt's letter also indicates the default drive. The default drive is the disk drive that DOS goes to automatically if you do not type a drive specification. On a single or dual drive system, the default drive is usually A>; on a hard disk system, the default drive is usually C>. Simply typing the drive letter followed by a colon overrides the default. If you intend to perform a number of operations on the files in the drive which is not the default, you may wish to change the default disk drive. In **THE MICROCOMPUTING SERIES** all drive specifications are indicated.

STARTUP PROCEDURES IF MICROCOMPUTER SYSTEM IS TURNED OFF

Single or Dual Drive System

1. The door on Disk Drive A should be open. Insert the DOS disk or a program disk on which DOS has been installed.

2. When the disk is fully inserted, close the drive door.

3. If you have dual disk drives and have a second disk for data, insert it into Disk Drive B.

4. When the disk is fully inserted, close the drive door.

5. Make sure that the printer is turned on and that the power, ready, and online lights (or their equivalent) are on.

6. Turn on the power switch.

7. When the red in-use disk drive lights go off, the program should be loaded.

8. Adjust the contrast controls on the monitor to a comfortable level.

9. If you have a single disk drive and a data disk, remove the program disk from Drive A.

10. Insert the data disk into Drive A.

11. When the disk is fully inserted, close the drive door.

Hard Disk System

1. Make sure that the printer is turned on and that the power, ready, and online lights (or their equivalent) are on.

2. Turn on the power switch.

3. When the red in-use disk drive lights go off, the program should be loaded.

4. Adjust the contrast controls on the monitor to a comfortable level.

5. After the program has loaded, you may insert a data disk into Drive A.

STARTUP PROCEDURES IF MICROCOMPUTER SYSTEM IS TURNED ON

Single or Dual Drive System

1. Adjust the contrast controls on the monitor.

2. The door on Disk Drive A should be open. Insert the DOS disk or a program that has been set up with DOS.

3. When the disk is fully inserted, close the drive door.

4. If you have a second disk for data, insert it into Disk Drive B.

5. When the disk is fully inserted, close the drive door.

6. Make sure that the printer is turned on and that the power, ready, and online lights (or their equivalent) are on.

7. Load the program by pressing and holding the Ctrl + Alt keys; then press the <DEL> key. RELEASE ALL THREE KEYS.

8. When the red in-use disk drive lights go off, the program should be loaded. Continue with the procedures related to the program being used.

Hard Disk System

1. Make sure that the printer is turned on and that the power, ready, and online lights (or their equivalent) are on.

2. Load the program. Press and hold the Ctrl + the Alt keys; then touch the <DEL> key. RELEASE ALL THREE KEYS.

3. When the red in-use disk drive lights go off, the program should be loaded.

4. Adjust the contrast controls on the monitor.

5. After the program has loaded, you may insert a data disk into Drive A.

6. Continue with the procedures related to the program being used.

SETTING THE DATE AND TIME

It is strongly recommended that you allow the system to "time stamp" the files you are using by setting the date and time whenever you begin a work session. (Some microcomputers have special boards with clocks that automatically set the time. If your system has this feature, you may skip these procedures.)

1. When DOS asks for the current date, type the current date using one of the following formats: xx/xx/xx or xx-xx-xx. Fill in appropriate numbers where x's appear. Do not type the name of the day; this would result in an "invalid date" prompt. (For example: April 30, 1986 is entered as "4-30-86" or "4/30/86".)

2. Press <CR>.

3. When DOS asks for the time, type the current time using this format: xx:xx. Fill in appropriate numbers where x's appear using 24-hour time to distinguish a.m. from p.m. Do not type "a.m." or "p.m." (For example, 10:15 a.m. is simply typed as "10:15" -- no other time indicators are required. If you are starting at 1:15 in the afternoon, you would type "13:15".)

4.   Press <CR>.

The DOS prompt will appear on the screen ("A>" with a single or dual drive system or "C>" with a hard disk).

Resetting the Date

If you enter the wrong date or forget to enter the date at system startup or reset, you can reset the date with the Date command:

1.   Type "Date".

2.   Press <CR>.

3.   Type in the appropriate date according to the format discussed above.

Resetting the Time

If you enter the wrong time or forget to enter the time at system startup or reset, you can reset the time with the Time command.

1.   Type "Time".

2.   Press <CR>.

3.   Type in the appropriate time according to the format discussed above.

SHUTDOWN PROCEDURES

1.   Make sure that you have followed the proper escape or exit procedures for the software program you are using. Failure to follow such precautions may result in lost data.

2.   When the red in-use disk drive lights are off for both drives, remove the disk from one of the drives. Do not close the drive door.

3.   Follow the same procedure and remove the disk from the other drive. Do not close the drive door.

4.   If you know that you or someone else will be using the system within a short time, leave the system turned on in order to minimize wear and tear. In order to protect your display, however, turn down the contrast.

PART III: ISSUING COMMANDS

TO ISSUE COMMANDS

1. The command must be typed exactly as described in this appendix, including any spaces within the command.

2. Commands may be typed in upper- or lower-case letters. DOS reads them as upper-case letters.

3. If the command you type contains a typographical error, a missing space, or an extra space, the prompt "Bad Command or File Name" appears after you press <CR>. If this prompt appears, simply retype the command correctly.

4. Be sure to press <CR> after you have typed in any command in order to tell the system to begin the procedure.

TO CORRECT A TYPING MISTAKE BEFORE YOU TOUCH <CR>

1.   The <BACKSPACE> key may be used to correct errors made while in DOS. Characters are erased as you backspace. The <Left> arrow also moves the cursor to the left; however, characters are not erased as the cursor moves to the left.

2. If a line has many errors, just touch the <ESC> key. A backslash (\) will appear. The cursor moves down one line on the screen, and even though the error-filled line still appears on the screen, it is deleted from memory. The system then waits for your corrected command.

TO STOP A COMMAND IN PROGRESS

1. Hold down the Ctrl + <BREAK> keys.

    The Break key has "Scroll Lock" on the top and "Break" on the forward edge.

2. Release both keys. Execution of the command will halt.

3. The system command ("A>" or "C>") will reappear and you can type your next command.

PARAMETERS

Parameters are items that can be included in DOS command statements in order to specify additional information to the system. Some parameters are required, others are optional. If you do not include some parameters, a default value is provided by the system.   Examples of some of the parameters you will be working with frequently when using DOS follow.

Parameter	Explanation
[filespec]	A filespec will appear as [d:][filename][.ext] Example: B:myfile.doc A:yourfile anyfiles.bas thisfile An explanation of each part of the filespec follows.
[d:]	This parameter is the drive indicator. Enter the drive letter followed by a colon to indicate the intended drive. For example to do a directory of the disk in Drive B (when B is not the default drive), type "Dir B:". After you press <CR>, the system displays the directory of the disk in drive B. If you do not specify a drive in the command, the system assumes that the default drive is intended. For example, if the default drive is Drive A, type "Dir". When you press <CR>, the system gives you a directory of the disk in Drive A.
[filename]	You may assign any name to a file as long as it meets the following criteria: The name assigned to the file can have from one to eight characters. Valid characters: A to Z 0 to 9 $ & @ % / \ _ - () '' {} # ! The filename parameters are in force even when you are using application software, but some software does not accept all the characters listed above.
[.ext]	You may assign an optional filename extension of from one to three characters. If you specify the optional three-character extension, it must be separated from the filename by a period. Sometimes you cannot specify the filename extension because the application program does so automatically. Again, the characters listed are the only valid characters. If an extension is assigned, you must include it as part of the filespec whenever you want the system to locate the file.

CHANGE DEFAULT DRIVE

Change the default drive to B>

1. Type "B:".

2. Press <CR>.

Change the default drive to A>

1. Type "A:".

2. Press <CR>.

Change the default drive to C>

1. Type "C:".

2. Press <CR>.

    The last command does not work unless you have a hard disk drive or some other special configuration.

CHECKDISK

The Checkdisk command produces a disk and memory status report. The report tells you how much space your files are using on the disk, how much space is still available on the disk, and whether the disk has any bad sectors (if a disk does have bad sectors, you may want to use the Copy *.* command to copy all your files to another formatted disk). Checkdisk also indicates how much memory is available in the system unit you are using.

1. The DOS disk should be in the default drive (either A> or C>) and the disk to be checked should be in Drive B (single or dual drive system) or Drive C (hard disk).

2. Type "Chkdsk B:", "Chkdsk A:" or "Chkdsk C:".

3. Press <CR>.

COPY

The Copy command allows you to transfer a copy of files from one disk to another without erasing any data on the disk to which you are copying. This is one method that can be used to back up your data disks.

The disk that contains the files you wish to copy is called the **source disk**. The disk to which you are copying is called the **target** or **destination disk**.

In order to use this command, the target disk must already have been formatted. The name of the file to be copied must be spelled correctly and the complete filespec (drive designation [if not default drive], file name, and any optional extension) must be included.

1. DOS must be loaded.

2. Place the source disk in one of the drives and the target disk in the other drive.

3. Type "Copy", enter the source drive and filename, and then enter the target drive. The command is executed by <CR>.

    a. If the file you wish to copy is in Drive A and the target disk is in Drive B, type the command as follows:

        "Copy A:filename.ext B:"

        Since the new filename is not specified, DOS assumes that you want the filename to stay the same.

    b. If the file you wish to copy is in Drive B and the target disk is in Drive A, type the command as follows:

        "Copy B:filename.ext A:"

        Since a new filename is not specified, DOS assumes that you want the filename to stay the same.

    c. If the file you wish to copy is in Drive C (root directory) and the target disk is in Drive A, type the command as follows:

        "Copy C:filename.ext A:"

        Since a new filename is not specified, DOS assumes that you want the filename to stay the same.

    With any form of the command, you are specifying that you want to copy the named file from the first drive designated to the disk located in the second drive indicated.

4. If the system cannot find the file, it indicates "0 Files copies." Check the spelling of the filename. Be sure you have included any extension that has been assigned to the file. If you made a mistake in typing the command, just retype it at the DOS prompt as described previously.

COPY USING GLOBAL CHARACTER (*)

When you wish to copy more than one file and there is some common element in the names of the files you wish to copy, you can use the global character (*) to expedite the process.

1. DOS should be loaded.

2. Remove the DOS disk from Drive A.

3. Insert the source and target disks into the disk drives.

    a. If the source disk is in Drive A, the target disk is in Drive B, and the files you wish to copy have the extension in common, type

        "Copy A:*.ext B:"

        Press <CR>.

        Since a new filename is not specified, DOS assumes that you want the filename to stay the same.

    b. If the source disk is in Drive B, the target disk is in Drive A, and the files you wish to copy have the extension in common, type

        "Copy B:*.ext A:"

        Press <CR>.

        Since a new filename is not specified, DOS assumes that you want the filename to stay the same.

    c. If the source disk is in Drive C (root directory), the target disk is in Drive A, and the files you wish to copy have the extension in common, type

        "Copy C:*.ext A:"

        Press <CR>.

        Since a new filename is not specified, DOS assumes you want the filename to stay the same.

    d. If the source disk is in Drive A, the target disk is in Drive B, and the files you wish to copy have the filename in common, type

        "Copy A:filename.* B:"

        Press <CR>.

e.   If the source disk is in Drive B, the target disk is in Drive A, and the files you wish to copy have the filename in common, type

"Copy B:filename.* A:"

Press <CR>.

f.   If the source disk is in Drive C (root directory), the target disk is in Drive A, and the files you wish to copy have the filename in common, type

"Copy C:filename.* A:"

Press <CR>.

4.   If the system cannot find the files, it indicates "0 Files copies." Check the spelling of the filename. Be sure you have included any extension assigned to the file. If you made a mistake in typing the command, just retype it at the DOS prompt as described previously.

COPY *.* (File by file)

With this command you copy the entire contents of the source disk onto a formatted target disk without erasing any data on the target disk.

1.   DOS must be loaded.

2.   Remove the DOS disk from Drive A.

3.   Insert the source disk and the target disk in the drives.

a.   If the source disk is in Drive A and the target disk is in Drive B, type

"Copy A: *.* B:"

Press <CR>.

b.   If the source disk is in Drive B and the target disk is in Drive A, type

"Copy B: *.* A:"

Press <CR>.

c.   If the source disk is in Drive A and the target disk is Drive C, type

"Copy A: *.* C:"

Press <CR>.

4. When the copy is complete, the number of files copied appears on the screen (or a message that there is insufficient disk space).

DELETE (ERASE FILE)

This command is used to delete a specified file from a disk in the designated drive.

1. DOS must be loaded, but the DOS disk does not have to be in the drive when the command is given.

2. Make sure the disk containing the file to be deleted is in the drive before you press <CR>.

    a. If the disk containing the file(s) to be deleted is in Drive B, type

        "Del B:filename.ext" or "Erase B:filename.ext"

        Press <CR>.

    b. If the disk containing the file(s) to be deleted is in Drive A, type

        "Del A:filename.ext" or "Erase A:filename.ext"

        Press <CR>.

    c. If the disk containing the file(s) to be deleted is in Drive C, type

        "Del C:filename.ext" or "Erase C:filename.ext"

        Press <CR>.

3. If the file is successfully erased, there is no message. The global character can be used with the Delete (or Erase) command just as it was used with the Copy command. However, the file-by-file delete is not recommended. Formatting is the preferred method of erasing all files from a floppy disk.

4. If the system cannot find the file, it gives you an error message. Check the spelling of the filename. Be sure you have included any extension that has been assigned to the file. If you made a mistake in typing the command, just retype it at the DOS prompt.

DIRECTORY

The directory is a listing of all files located on the disk in the specified drive. It is possible to display a directory on a disk in any drive in the system.

1. DOS must be loaded.

    a. If you wish to see a directory on the disk in Drive B, type

        "Dir B:"

        Press <CR>.

    b. If you wish to see a directory on the disk in Drive A, type

        "Dir A:"

        Press <CR>.

    c. If you wish to see a directory of the disk in Drive C, type

        "Dir C:"

        Press <CR>.

        A listing of the names of the files located on the disk in the designated drive will appear.

DIRECTORY (PAUSE)

With this form of the Directory command, the listing pauses so that you can read the first lines of the directory. When you are ready, press any key to continue the listing.

1. Type "Dir/P A:", "Dir/P B:", or "Dir/P C:".

2. Press <CR>.

DIRECTORY (WIDE)

This form of the Directory command produces a wide display that lists only the file names.

1. Type "Dir/W A:", "Dir/W B:", or "Dir/W C:".

2. Press <CR>.

DIRECTORY (PRINT)

If you would like to print the directory rather than have it appear on screen, use the following command.

1. Type "Dir A:>Prn", "Dir B:>Prn", or "Dir C:>Prn".

2. Press <CR>.

    The directory will print.

DISKCOPY

With the Diskcopy command you can copy the entire contents of a disk onto another disk. The Diskcopy command also formats the target disk. Be careful when you use this command; any files on the target disk will be erased.

1. Type "Diskcopy A: B:" or "Diskcopy B: A:".

2. Press <CR>.

TO STOP THE SCREEN FROM SCROLLING

Information sometimes appears on the screen and then scrolls off before you can read it, as frequently happens when you display a long directory. The following procedure stops the scrolling until you are ready for it to continue.

1. Press the Ctrl + <NUM LOCK> keys.

2. Release both keys.

    The scrolling will stop.

3. Press any key to restart the scrolling.

FORMAT

The Format command can be used to format a blank disk (a disk cannot be used on the system until it is formatted) or to erase an entire disk that contains data you no longer need (such a disk can then be reused). Unless you wish to use the Format command to erase a disk, you will have to format each disk only once.

Caution. This command erases the entire contents of disk. If you have any doubts about the contents of the disk you are going to format, display a directory of the disk to make sure that it does not contain any files you want to keep (see Directory in this appendix).

1. DOS should be loaded and the DOS disk should be in Drive A.

2. Type "Format B:".

3. Press <CR>.

4. When the system prompts you to insert a new disk in the designated drive, make sure that the disk you wish to format is in the designated drive.

5. Touch any key to begin the formatting process.

6. When the formatting process is complete, you will be asked if you wish to format another disk. If you wish to format another disk, type the letter "Y" for "yes" and follow the screen prompts to insert a blank disk. If you do not wish to format another disk, type the letter "N" for "no." Your data disk is now ready to be used with the system.

FORMAT WITH VOLUME LABEL

By using the V option of the Format command you put an electronic label on your disk. When you use the Directory or Checkdisk commands, this electronic volume label is displayed.

1. DOS should be loaded and the DOS disk should be in Drive A. A blank disk should be in Drive B.

2. Type "Format B:/V".
3. Press <CR>.

4. When the system prompts you to insert a new disk in the designated drive, make sure that the disk you wish to format is in the designated drive.

5. Touch any key to begin the formatting process.

6. Part of the process will be completed when the following appears on the screen:

```
Formatting...Format complete

Volume label (11 characters, ENTER for none)?
```

7. Type in the label you want to use, for example, your name, social security number, or the disk number. Review the filename parameters for a list of valid characters.

8. Press <CR>.

9. When the formatting process is complete, you will be asked if you wish to format another disk. If you wish to format another disk, type the letter "Y" for "yes" and follow the screen prompts to insert a blank disk. If you do not wish to format another disk, type the letter "N" for "no." Your data disk is now ready to be used with the system.

PRINT SCREEN FUNCTION

The Print Screen function is available through DOS. It allows you to print an exact copy of what appears on the screen.

1. Be sure DOS is loaded and the printer is turned on and is on line.

2. Press the Shift-<PrtSc> keys.

3. Release both keys.

    The contents of the screen will print.

OUTPUT TO PRINTER FUNCTION

When the Output to Printer or Echo function is activated, anything that is typed on the keyboard appears on both the screen and on paper.

1. Be sure DOS is loaded.

2. Make sure that the printer is turned on and is on line.

3. Press and hold the Ctrl key and then just touch the <PrtSc> key. When you use these keys to activate the Output to Printer function, it will appear that nothing has happened.

4. Release both keys.

5. In order to see if the function has been activated, press the <CR> key a few times. The paper will advance one line and print the command prompt (e.g., "A>") each time you press <CR>.

6. If there is no printer response, repeat the procedure.

HOW TO DEACTIVATE OUTPUT TO PRINTER

Until you deactivate the Output to Printer function, everything that appears on the display will also appear on paper.

1. Make sure the printer is on line. Press the Ctrl-<PrtSc> keys.

2. Release both keys.

3. This stops the output to the printer. In order to be sure that the function is no longer active, press the <CR> key a few times. If the paper does not advance one line and print the command prompt each time you press <CR>, the Output to Printer function is deactivated.

APPENDIX

B ANSWERS TO CHECKPOINT QUESTIONS

Unit 2

a. B> will appear
b. Drive B
c. to end one line and begin another; to create blank lines
d. 19 (if the left margin is set at 10)
e. 9 (if typing began on Ln 1 and a <CR> was inserted between paragraphs)
f. F10
g. <Home>, <Down> arrow keys
h. <Home>, <Home>, <Up> arrow keys
i. <Down> arrow key; twice
j. <Home>, <Home>, <Down> arrow keys
k. <Up> arrow key
l. <Right> arrow key
m. Ctrl-<Right> arrow keys; four times
n. <Home>, <Home>, <Right> arrow keys
o. <Home>, <Home>, <Left> arrow keys
p. F7
q. Your revised document can be saved in the original file or placed it in a new file with a new filename.
r. Shift-F10

UNIT 3

a. <CR>
b. 3
c. <DEL>
d. Ctrl-<End>
e. 25
f. Retrieve the document, press Shift-F7, type "1"

UNIT 4

a. the number next to Pos appears in a contrasting color or intensity
b. F8
c. F6
d. <CAPS LOCK>
e. Shift-F6
f. press <CR>
g. it jumped to the right margin
h. Alt-F4
i. the text appears in a contrasting color or intensity; the change is indicated in the status line
j. the text appears in a contrasting color or intensity; the change is indicated in the status line
k. Block, Ctrl-F4, option 1, move the cursor to the new location, Ctrl-F4, option 5
l. Alt-F4, Shift-F3
m. highlight the period from the preceding sentence before turning on the Switch feature
n. Alt-F3
o. [C],[U]
p. [A],[a]
q. [U],[B]

UNIT 5

Section 1
a. the Print Format menu
b. 12
c. press <CR>

Section 2
a. Shift-F8
b. text is formatted within the new margin settings
c. Shift-F8, 1
d. move the cursor to the first tab stop, press Ctrl-<End>
e. F7
f. Shift-F8, 4, 1.5
g. The text appears double-spaced on the screen. The Ln number in the status line identifies the line on which the cursor is resting.

Section 3
a. Alt-F8
b. select 3 after choosing a header from the Header/Footer Specification submenu
c. Alt-F8, 1, select an option from the Position of Page Number of Page submenu
d. Alt-F8, A, Y
e. Alt-F8, 3

UNIT 6

a. Shift-F7
b. press Shift-F7, type "3", type "2", type "2"
c. press Shift-F7, type "2"
d. Alt-F4
e. 1
f. Shift-F7, 4, S
g. type "G" from the Printer Control submenu
h. Shift-F7, 4, P, document name, select starting page, select ending page
i. "Starting page" and "Ending page" prompts after the document selection allow you to select specific pages to be printed
j. type "C" from the Printer Control submenu

UNIT 7

a. Shift-F5
b. name of month, the date, and the year
c. F4
d. it is indented from both margins
e. F4, Shift-<TAB>
f. <ESC>
g. <ESC>, type number after the prompt, type character
h. Shift-F1
i. a lower case "s"
j. option 5, (Adv Dn)
k. F2
l. a "Not found" message appears on the screen
m. Shift-F2
n. Alt-F2, N
o. Ctrl-F3, 1, answer the prompt, "# Lines in this Window"
p. press Ctrl-F3, type "1", answer the prompt by typing a number greater than the number of lines on the screen (e.g., >24)

UNIT 9

a. read prompt at page bottom
b. option 1

UNIT 10

a. F9
b. Shift-F9
c. Alt-F9

d. Ctrl-F9
e. a message is displayed to remind you of the information you would like to enter from the keyboard
f. the printer pauses
g. information from the second field in a record is entered into the document
h. measure from the top of one label to the top of the next label
i. at one line
j. the Line Format menu

UNIT 11

a. Ctrl-F10
b. press Ctrl-F10 again
c. when the prompt "Macro Def" appears on the screen
d. when the "Define Macro" message appears on the screen, hold down the Alt key while typing a single letter from A-Z
e. press Alt-F10, then type the name of the macro file
f. press Alt and the file letter
g. Ctrl-F10
h. Ctrl-F10

UNIT 12

a. from the Text Column Definition submenu, type "N" after the prompt "Do you want groups kept together on a page? (Y/N) N"
b. select option 3 from the Math/Columns menu
c. Ctrl-<CR>
d. from the Text Column Definition submenu, type "Y" after the prompt "Do you want groups of information kept together on a page? Y/N N"

UNIT 13

a. Alt-F5
b. Block the text for each heading
c. option 7 from the Mark Text menu (Block off)

UNIT 14

a. Alt-F7
b. type "2" in the Type row on the Math Definition submenu
c. it automatically jumps to Calculation Formulas on the Math Definition submenu
d. F7
e. the first one
f. by selecting option 1 from the Math/Columns menu
g. "!" appears in the calculation column
h. subtotals above the operator in the numeric column are added
i. option 2 from the Math/Columns [Math on] menu
j. Alt-F7, option 1

APPENDIX

C

WORDPERFECT VERSION 4.2

WordPerfect 4.2 is designed with changes that enhance several of the features included in WordPerfect 4.1. This supplement describes the updated features of WordPerfect 4.2 that affect the text of the <u>Understanding and Using WordPerfect</u> workbook. The updated features are described and cross-referenced with the original text. If you use the explanations in this supplement instead of the explanations in the original text, you will have no difficulty understanding and using WordPerfect 4.2.

THE STATUS LINE
(p. 14, first paragraph under topic heading; p.15, FIGURE 2-1)

The status line (Figure C-1) is displayed at the bottom of the screen. The status line states (from left to right) the current filename, including the full pathname, the current document number and page number, line number, and column (position) number at which the cursor is presently located. This filename is temporarily replaced whenever a message from the program of from DOS is displayed.

```
┌──────────────────────────────────────────────────────────────────┐
│                                                                    │
│  A:\FORFUN                                    Doc 1  Pg 1  Ln 1  Pos 10 │
│                                                                    │
└──────────────────────────────────────────────────────────────────┘
```

FIGURE C-1 Clear Screen with Status Line.

HARD PAGE
(p. 16, first paragraph)

To end a page before it is filled with text, press the Ctrl-<CR> keys. A line of
equal signs (=) appears on the screen to indicate the end of one page and the
beginning of another. The cursor jumps to the new page. If you want to delete
this hard page break, move the cursor below the page break line and press
<BACKSPACE>.

IMPORTANT KEYSTROKES
(p. 28)

Add the following keystrokes to the list:

10. Home, <BACKSPACE>.......to delete characters left of the cursor to the word
                           boundary

If you have incorrectly typed several characters in a word, you can backspace
and, therefore delete all those characters with two keystrokes, Home,
<BACKSPACE>.

11. Home, <DEL>............to delete characters right of the cursor to the work
                           boundary

If you are editing a word, and several unwanted characters remain at the end of
the word you are editing, you can delete all those characters with two
keystrokes, Home, <DEL>.

REVEAL CODES
(p. 54, third paragraph under topic heading)

When you press the Alt-F3 keys, the screen is split in two by the Tab Ruler. The
upper window displays normal text; the lower window displays the text along with
the hidden codes. It is easy to distinguish between text and codes in the lower
window, because all codes are boldfaced. Text, however is never boldfaced nor
underlined in the lower window. The cursor in the lower window is also
boldfaced. It blinks at a different rate from the cursor in the normal text
screen. Each window displays three lines of text above the blinking cursor.

TABS
(p. 70, FIGURE 5-3; p. 71, FIGURE 5-4; p. 70 & 71, explanation of options 1 & 2 on the Line Format menu, explanation of the Tabs Setting submenu; p. 74, GUIDED ACTIVITY; CHANGING TAB SETTINGS)

1 2 Tabs; 3 Margins; 4 Spacing; 5 Hyphenation; 6 Align Char: 0

FIGURE C-2   Line Format Menu.

The Line Format menu options are defined as follows:

1 2 Tabs   The Tabs Setting submenu (Figure C-3) appears on the screen. The cursor on this submenu appears in the same position it was in the text. Tabs are preset at five-space intervals.

```
L....L....L....L....L....L....L....L....L....L....L....L....L....L....L.
0123456789012345678901234567890123456789012345678901234567890123456789012345678
        20        30        40        50        60        70        80
Delete EOL (clear tabs); Enter number (set tab); Del (clear tab);

Left; Center; Right; Decimal; .= Dot leader; Press EXIT when done.
```

FIGURE C-3   Tabs Setting Submenu.

The Tabs Setting submenu:

To clear all previous tab settings, move the cursor to the first tab and press the Ctrl-<End> keys.

To delete one tab, move the cursor to the tab set on the ruler and press <DEL>.

To set multiple left-justified tab stops, type the column number for the first tab stop, type "," (comma), then the interval number. (L) is the default tab setting.

To set multiple right-justified tab stops, type "R", type the column number for the first tab stop, type "," (comma), then the interval number.

To set multiple tab stops that align decimal points, type "D", type the column number for the first tab stop, type "," (comma), then the interval number.

To set multiple tab stops that center text, type "C", type the column number for the first tab stop, type "," (comma), then the interval number.

To set a single tab stop, move the cursor to the desired column position, then type the appropriate letter (i.e.,"L", "R", "D", or "C". Because the default tab setting is L, you can also set a left-justified tab stop by simply typing the desired position number and pressing <CR>.

To include a dot leader with left, right and decimal aligned text, move the cursor to the L,R, or D and type a "." (period) over the letter.

To exit the Tabs Setting submenu, press F7.

Tabs may be set up to position 250, but after position 40, only left-justified (L) tabs may be set. Use the cursor (horizontal) movement keys to move the cursor across the Tabs Setting submenu.

GUIDED ACTIVITY: CHANGING TAB SETTINGS

1.   Display a clear screeen.

2.   Press the Shift-F8 keys.

The Line Format menu will appear.

3.   Type 1 or 2.

The Tabs Setting submenu will appear.

4.   Position the cursor over column 10 on the Tabs Setting submenu.

5.   Press the Ctrl-<End> keys.

All of the tabs from the cursor forward have been deleted.

6.   Type "15".

7.   Press <CR>.

The first left-justified tab stop has been set at Pos 15.

8.   Type "35".

9.   Press <CR>.

     A left-justified tab stop has been set at Pos 35.

10. Type "55".

11. Press <CR>.

     A left-justified tab stop has been set at Pos 55.

12. Type "65".

13. Press <CR>.

     A left-justified tab stop has been set at Pos 65.

14. Press F7 to Exit the Tabs Setting submenu.

THE DATE AND TIME FEATURE
(p. 113, Figure 7-2 Format Submenu)

```
Date Format

     Number          Meaning
        1               Day of the Month
        2               Month (number)
        3               Month (word)
        4               Year (all four digits)
        5               Year (last two digits)
        6               Day of the week (word)
        7               Hour (24 Hour Clock)
        8               Hour (12 Hour Clock)
        9               Minute
        0               am / pm
        %               Include leading zero for number less than 10
                            (must directly precede number)

Examples:        3 1, 4     =December 25, 1984
                 %2/%1/5    =01/01/85 (Tuesday)


Date Format      3 1, 4
```

FIGURE C-4 Format Submenu.

THE THESAURUS
(p. 158, first paragraph under topic heading)

The WordPerfect Thesaurus helps you choose exactly the right words as you create your documents.   It displays a list of nouns, verbs, and adjectives that are similar in meaning to the words you might want to revise.   The Thesaurus also displays a list of antonymns, words that are opposite in meaning to the words you might want to revise.   You can either direct the Thesaurus to automatically replace a word or to keep the word you originally typed.

(p. 159, explanation of special terms, "1 Headword")

1 Headword.   A headword is a word that can be looked up in the Thesaurus. If you see the message "Word not found", it means that the word you want to look up is not listed.

TEXT COLUMNS
(p. 196, third paragraph under topic heading)

Two to twenty-four text columns can be defined across a page.   Defining columns is much like setting margins, except that the task is done automatically.   Margin calculations are based on the current margin settings of your document.   The column format you have defined appears on the screen as well as on the printed document.   You may, however, display each column on a separate page instead of side-by-side by using the column display option on the Math/Columns menu.

(p.197, Figure 12-2)

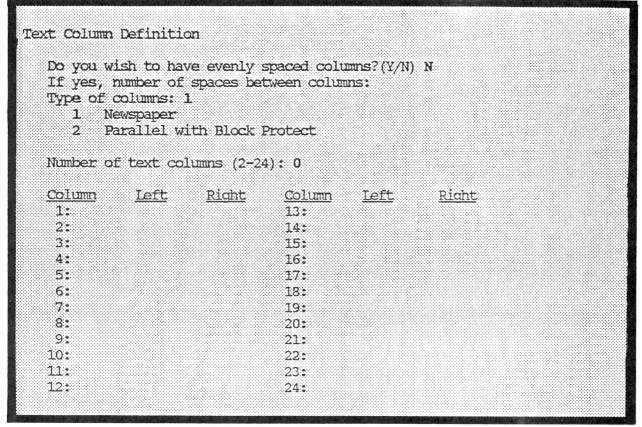

FIGURE C-5   Text Column Definition Submenu.

(p. 197, Guidelines for defining text columns: third paragraph)

To set up newspaper or parallel columns, select the appropriate number (1 or 2) after the prompt "Type of Columns: 1".

(p. 198, GUIDED ACTIVITY: CREATING A NEWSPAPER COLUMN)   Follow steps 1-7 in original text; then replace steps 8-11 with steps 8-10 on this page. Continue with steps 12-21 to create newspaper columns.

8.   Press <CR> after the prompt "Type of Columns: 1".

     You have selected newspaper-style columns.

9.   Type "2" after the prompt "Number of text columns (2-24).

     The margins for two text columns will be automatically calculated and then displayed in the Column margin table on the Text Column Definition submenu.

10. Press Exit to return to the Math/Columns menu screen.

(p.199, GUIDED ACTIVITY: CREATING PARALLEL COLUMNS) Replace step 7 with the following step:

7.   Type "2" to select parallel-style columns.

INDEX

A

Advance down, 119, 122
Advance up, 119
Align character, 72
Append to File, 52
Arrow keys, 18

B

Backspace, 31
Backup, 57
Block and Switch, 52
Block text, 48
Boldface, 44

C

Calculation columns, 213, 214
Cancel a print job, 107
Cancel key, 21
Capitalization, 44

Carriage Return, 15
Center text horizontally, 45
Center page vertically, 87
Check menu, 154
Columns, 167-173
Conditional End of Page, 83
Copy blocks of text 43, 63
Copy for backup, 57
Copy, select number for printing, 101, 103
Cursor, horizontal movement, 18
Cursor, vertical movement, 18

D

Date menu, 112
Default values, 112
Delete a file, 141
Directory, change, 138
Double Word submenu, 156

E

Endnotes, 129
Exit WordPerfect, 20

F

File management, 137-142
Flush Right, 47
Footers, 81
Footnotes 129, 130
Format a disk, 13
Format key, 63
Format line, 70
Format, Print Format menu, 63
Format submenu, 113
Format, text, 62

G

Go To key, 20

H

Hanging paragraph, 116
Hard disk, 14
Hard page, 16
Hard space, 15
Headers, 81, 84
Help function, 22
Hyphenation, 72

I

Indenting, 115
Index, 205
Insert key, 32
Insert mode, 32

J

Job List, 102, 103

L

Line Format menu, 70
Line spacing, 72, 76
List Files menu, 139
Locked documents, 142

M

Macros, 179-186
Mailing labels, 172
Margin Release, 74
Margins, 71, 72, 81
Math, 211-220
Math/Columns menu, 196, 212
Math Definition submenu, 213
Mark Text menu, 204
Menus, 5, 50
Merging, 164-176
Move a block of text, 51
Move and Retrieve menu, 51
Move menu, 50

N

Name a document, 17
Newspaper columns, 197
Not Found submenu, 155
Numeric columns, 213

O

Outline, 205

P

Page centering, 80, 87
Page Format menu, 79
Page length, 80
Page numbering, 80, 85, 86
Parallel columns, 199
Pitch, 64, 66
Primary file, 167-169
Printing, 100
Printing a block of text, 104

Printing a document stored
  on a data disk, 106, 140
Print, change print options, 101
Printer control, 101, 102
Print Format menu, 63
Print menu, 100

Q

Quick Reference Card, 5

R

Redline, 205
Rename files, 139
Repeat a character or feature, 117
Replace, 125, 127
Retrieve, 23, 140
Rewrite feature, 32
Reveal codes, 54, 56
Right justification, 64, 67

S

Save a document, 16, 17
Save and Exit, 20
Screen menu, 133
Search and Replace, 123, 127
Search for text 123
Secondary file, 164-166, 175
Soft page, 15
Speller, 153-158
Split screens, 133
Status line, 14
Subscript, 119, 120
Superscript, 119, 120
Switch feature, 52

T

Tab, 32
Table of contents feature, 203-208
Tabs, extended, 71
Tab Ruler, 131-133
Tabs Setting submenu, 71
Template, 4

Text columns, 196
Text Marking Definition submenu, 206
Text In, 139
Thesaurus, 158-160
Toggle keys, 32
Typeover, 32

U

Undelete, 34
Underline, 44, 64
User's manual, 5

W

Widow/Orphan lines, 83, 86
Word Pattern, 155
Word Search, 140

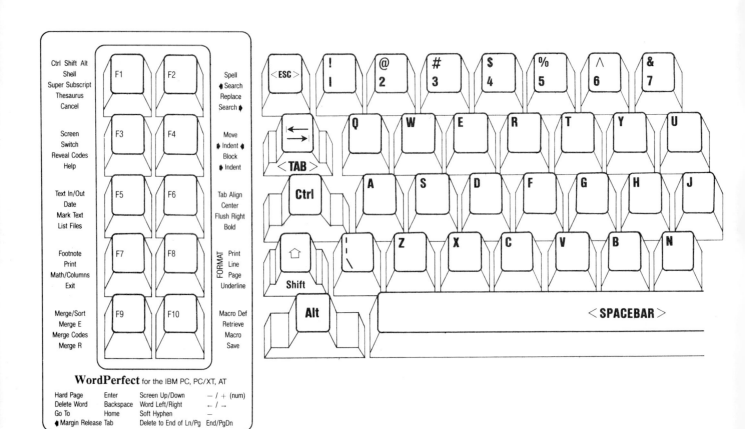

WordPerfect for the IBM PC, PC/XT, AT

Ctrl Shift Alt		Spell
Shell		◆ Search
Super Subscript		Replace
Thesaurus		Search ◆
Cancel		
Screen		Move
Switch		◆ Indent ◆
Reveal Codes		Block
Help		◆ Indent
Text In/Out		Tab Align
Date		Center
Mark Text		Flush Right
List Files		Bold
Footnote		Print
Print		Line
Math/Columns	FORMAT	Page
Exit		Underline
Merge/Sort		Macro Def
Merge E		Retrieve
Merge Codes		Macro
Merge R		Save

Hard Page	Enter	Screen Up/Down	− / + (num)
Delete Word	Backspace	Word Left/Right	← / →
Go To	Home	Soft Hyphen	−
◆ Margin Release	Tab	Delete to End of Ln/Pg	End/PgDn

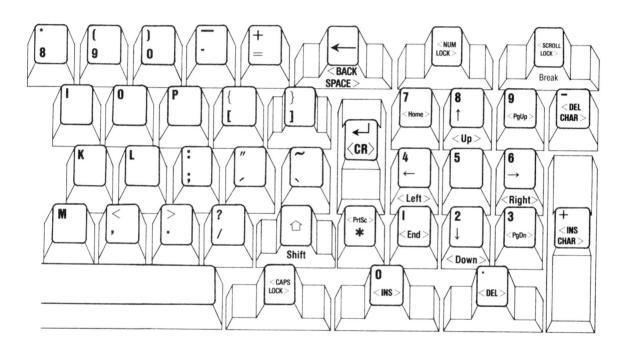

IBM PC™ Abbreviations

Esc—Escape Key	PrtSc—Print Screen Key
Ctrl—Control Key	Pg Dn—Page Down Key
Alt—Alternate Key	Ins— Insert Character
Num Lock—Number Lock Key	Del—Delete Character
Pg Up—Page Up Key	

Notes

Notes

Notes

Notes

Notes

Notes

Notes